I0409207

THE ONLINE MONEY PLAYBOOK

Mastering Advanced Online Money-Making Techniques

Shah Rukh

CONTENTS

INTRODUCTION

Welcome to "The Online Money Playbook: Mastering Advanced Online Money-Making Techniques." In today's digital age, the internet has transformed the way we live, work, and interact. It has also opened up incredible opportunities for individuals to generate income and build thriving businesses from the comfort of their own homes. This book is your comprehensive guide to navigating the dynamic world of online money-making, equipping you with the knowledge and strategies to unlock your full earning potential.

Whether you are a seasoned entrepreneur, a freelancer looking to expand your income streams, or someone seeking financial independence through online ventures, this book is designed to be your trusted companion on your journey to mastering advanced online money-making techniques. We will explore a diverse range of strategies, platforms, and tools that can propel you towards financial success in the digital realm.

The chapters in this book are carefully crafted to provide you with in-depth insights, practical tips, and actionable steps to excel in various online money-making avenues. From understanding the digital economy to choosing the right online money-making strategy, building a personal brand, monetizing blogs and websites, diving into affiliate marketing, creating information products, launching e-commerce stores, harnessing the power of social media, and exploring the world of cryptocurrencies, each chapter offers a comprehensive exploration of a specific topic.

Throughout the book, we emphasize the importance of cultivating a winning mindset, developing a customer-centric approach, building sustainable and scalable businesses, and continuously adapting to the ever-evolving digital landscape. We firmly believe that with the right knowledge, strategies, and dedication, anyone can tap into the vast potential of the online world and achieve financial freedom.

"The Online Money Playbook: Mastering Advanced Online Money-Making Techniques" is not just a theoretical guide; it is a practical roadmap that empowers you to take immediate action and implement proven strategies. Each chapter is packed with real-life examples, case studies, and expert insights to inspire and guide you on your path to success.

It's important to note that while the internet offers countless opportunities, online money-making requires effort, persistence, and a commitment to continuous learning. This book will equip you with the necessary tools and knowledge, but it's up to you to put them into practice and adapt them to your unique circumstances and aspirations.

As you embark on this transformative journey, remember that success rarely happens overnight. Building an online business and achieving financial independence is a process that requires patience, perseverance, and a willingness to learn from both successes and failures. The online world is constantly evolving, and embracing change and innovation will be key to your long-term success.

So, are you ready to dive into "The Online Money Playbook: Mastering Advanced Online Money-Making Techniques"? Prepare to unlock the doors to a world of opportunity, financial abundance, and personal freedom. Let's embark on this exciting adventure together and shape a future where the internet becomes your ultimate resource for creating the life you desire.

Let's get started!

CHAPTER 1: INTRODUCTION TO ADVANCED ONLINE MONEY-MAKING TECHNIQUES

In today's digital age, the internet has transformed the way we live, work, and make money. With the right knowledge and strategies, individuals can tap into the vast opportunities presented by the online world to generate significant income streams. This chapter serves as a comprehensive introduction to advanced online money-making techniques, equipping readers with the fundamental knowledge and mindset necessary to embark on their journey towards financial success.

1.1 The Evolution of Online Money-Making: The chapter begins by providing a historical overview of the evolution of online money-making. It explores how the internet has revolutionized traditional business models and opened up new avenues for generating income. From the early days of e-commerce to the rise of social media influencers and the emergence of the gig economy, readers gain a deeper understanding of the dynamic landscape of online entrepreneurship.

1.2 The Benefits and Challenges of Online Money-Making: Next, the chapter delves into the benefits and challenges associated with pursuing online money-making ventures. It highlights the flexibility, scalability, and global reach that online platforms offer, enabling individuals to reach a vast audience and operate businesses with minimal overhead costs. However, it also discusses the potential pitfalls, such as intense competition, rapid technological changes, and the need for continuous adaptation and learning.

1.3 Essential Mindset for Online Success: Building a solid foundation for success is crucial in any endeavor, and online money-making is no exception. This section explores the essential mindset characteristics necessary to thrive in the digital landscape. It emphasizes the importance of resilience, perseverance, adaptability, and a growth mindset. Readers learn to embrace challenges, view failures as learning opportunities, and cultivate a mindset that fuels their online success.

1.4 Key Principles of Advanced Online Money-Making Techniques: To navigate the vast realm of online money-making, it is essential to understand the key principles that underpin successful ventures. This section outlines the core principles, including identifying profitable niches, conducting market research, building a personal brand, leveraging digital marketing strategies, and diversifying income streams. By grasping these principles, readers gain a holistic perspective on the various aspects of advanced online money-making.

1.5 Exploring Different Online Money-Making Strategies: The chapter introduces readers to a wide array of advanced online money-making strategies. It covers diverse areas such as affiliate marketing, information product creation, e-commerce, social media marketing, influencer marketing, YouTube monetization, podcasting, online advertising, email marketing, cryptocurrency trading, investing, freelancing, and more. Each strategy is explained in detail, highlighting its potential, requirements, and best practices.

1.6 Crafting a Personalized Online Money-Making Plan: To succeed in the online realm, a customized and well-thought-out plan is essential. This section guides readers through the process of crafting their personalized online money-making plan. It covers goal setting, strategy selection, resource allocation, and creating a roadmap for achieving long-term success. Readers learn how to align their skills, interests, and passions with the most suitable online money-making strategies.

1.7 Overcoming Obstacles and Taking Action: The chapter concludes by addressing common obstacles that individuals may encounter on their online money-making journey. It provides insights into overcoming challenges such as self-doubt, fear of failure, information overload, and analysis paralysis. Readers are encouraged to take action, start small, and gradually build momentum towards their online money-making goals.

By the end of Chapter 1, readers are equipped with a solid understanding of the online money-making landscape, the mindset required for success, and a range of advanced techniques to explore. Armed with this knowledge, they are prepared to delve deeper into subsequent chapters, where they will dive into each technique in greater detail, learning strategies and tactics to master the art of making money online.

CHAPTER 2: UNDERSTANDING THE DIGITAL ECONOMY

In the modern world, the digital economy has become an integral part of our lives. It encompasses the vast network of digital platforms, technologies, and services that facilitate the exchange of goods, services, and information. This chapter provides a comprehensive exploration of the digital economy, its components, and its impact on various industries and individuals.

2.1 The Digital Transformation: To understand the digital economy, it is crucial to grasp the concept of digital transformation. This section delves into the transformational changes brought about by digital technologies, such as the internet, mobile devices, cloud computing, artificial intelligence, and big data. It highlights how these technologies have disrupted traditional business models, creating new opportunities for innovation, efficiency, and growth.

2.2 The Components of the Digital Economy: The digital economy comprises several key components, each playing a vital role in the overall ecosystem. This section provides an in-depth analysis of these components, including e-commerce platforms, digital marketplaces, online payment systems, social media networks, mobile applications, and digital advertising networks. Readers gain a comprehensive understanding of how these components interact and contribute to the digital economy's functioning.

2.3 The Growth of Online Consumer Behavior: One of the significant drivers of the digital economy is the shift in consumer behavior towards online channels. This section explores the factors that have influenced this shift, such as convenience, accessibility, and a wide range of choices. It delves into the rise of online shopping, the increasing prevalence of mobile commerce, and the impact of customer reviews and recommendations in shaping purchasing decisions.

2.4 Digital Disruption in Industries: The digital economy has caused disruption across various industries, reshaping the way businesses operate and creating new opportunities for growth. This section examines how industries such as retail, media and entertainment, transportation, finance, healthcare, and education have been transformed by digital technologies. Readers gain insights into the challenges and opportunities presented by this disruption and the strategies employed by successful organizations to thrive in the digital age.

2.5 The Gig Economy and Digital Labor Marketplaces: The digital economy has facilitated the rise of the gig economy, where individuals can offer their skills and services on digital platforms. This section explores the concept of the gig economy and its impact on the labor market. It discusses the emergence of digital labor marketplaces, such as freelancing platforms and crowdsourcing platforms, and their role in connecting individuals with businesses seeking specialized talent. Readers gain a deeper understanding of the opportunities and challenges associated with participating in the gig economy.

2.6 Data as the Currency of the Digital Economy: In the digital economy, data plays a pivotal role. This section examines the significance of data as the currency driving the digital economy. It explores how data is collected, analyzed, and utilized by businesses to gain insights, enhance customer experiences, and make informed decisions. It also delves into the challenges surrounding data privacy, security, and ethical considerations that arise in this data-driven landscape.

2.7 Global Implications and Digital Divides: The digital economy has global implications, shaping economies, societies, and individuals worldwide. This section discusses the digital divide, which refers to the unequal access to digital technologies and internet connectivity. It explores the social, economic, and developmental implications of the digital divide and examines efforts to bridge this gap and promote digital inclusion.

2.8 Future Trends and Opportunities: To conclude the chapter, a glimpse into the future of the digital economy is provided. This section highlights emerging trends such as artificial intelligence, blockchain technology, the Internet of Things (IoT), and virtual and augmented reality. Readers gain insights into the potential impact of these technologies on the digital economy and the new opportunities they may unlock.

By the end of Chapter 2, readers have a comprehensive understanding of the digital economy, its various components, and its impact on industries and individuals. This knowledge sets the foundation for exploring advanced online money-making techniques in subsequent chapters, as readers become well-equipped to navigate and leverage the digital landscape for financial success.

CHAPTER 3: CHOOSING THE RIGHT ONLINE MONEY-MAKING STRATEGY

In the vast and dynamic world of online money-making, selecting the right strategy is crucial for success. Chapter 3 delves into the process of choosing the most suitable online money-making strategy based on individual preferences, skills, resources, and market conditions. This chapter provides readers with a comprehensive framework to evaluate and select the strategy that aligns with their goals and maximizes their chances of financial success.

3.1 Assessing Personal Interests and Passions: A fundamental step in choosing the right online money-making strategy is assessing personal interests and passions. This section emphasizes the importance of pursuing ventures that align with one's passions, as it fosters motivation, resilience, and enjoyment. Readers are encouraged to reflect on their hobbies, skills, and areas of expertise to identify potential niches and opportunities within the online realm that resonate with their interests.

3.2 Evaluating Skills and Expertise: Building on the assessment of personal interests, this section focuses on evaluating skills and expertise. Readers are encouraged to identify their strengths, whether they lie in writing, graphic design, coding, marketing, teaching, or any other area. By recognizing their skills, individuals can identify online money-making strategies that leverage their existing abilities and provide avenues for growth and mastery.

3.3 Understanding Market Demand and Trends: To make informed decisions about online money-making strategies, it is essential to understand market demand and trends. This section guides readers through the process of conducting market research to identify profitable niches and assess the viability of different strategies. It explores tools and techniques to analyze market demand, competition, and emerging trends, enabling readers to make data-driven decisions.

3.4 Considerations of Time and Resources: Choosing the right online money-making strategy also requires considering one's available time and resources. This section helps readers evaluate their availability, commitment level, and financial resources. It discusses strategies that may require more significant time investments, such as content creation or building an e-commerce business, as well as strategies that allow for more flexibility, such as freelancing or affiliate marketing.

3.5 Balancing Short-term and Long-term Goals: Another important aspect of strategy selection is balancing short-term and long-term goals. This section encourages readers to define their financial objectives, whether they aim for immediate income generation or long-term wealth accumulation. It explores different strategies that offer varying time horizons for returns, such as launching an online store versus investing in stocks or cryptocurrencies.

3.6 Evaluating Risk Tolerance: Risk tolerance is a critical factor in choosing an online money-making strategy. This section helps readers assess their risk tolerance by considering factors such as financial stability, willingness to take risks, and tolerance for uncertainty. It explores strategies with different risk profiles, such as trading in volatile markets versus building a stable, long-term business, enabling readers to align their risk tolerance with their chosen path.

3.7 Exploring Multiple Streams of Income: Diversification of income streams is a prudent approach in the online money-making landscape. This section emphasizes the importance of exploring multiple strategies to mitigate risks and maximize earning potential. It introduces readers to the concept of multiple streams of income and provides examples of how different strategies can complement each other to create a robust and sustainable online business.

3.8 Adapting to Market Dynamics: The digital landscape is constantly evolving, requiring individuals to adapt their strategies to market dynamics. This section emphasizes the need for flexibility and continuous learning. It discusses the importance of monitoring trends, experimenting with new approaches, and adapting strategies based on changing market conditions. Readers learn to stay agile and responsive to maintain a competitive edge.

3.9 Seeking Guidance and Mentorship: Choosing the right online money-making strategy can be overwhelming, especially for beginners. This section encourages readers to seek guidance and mentorship from experienced individuals in their chosen field. It explores resources such as online communities, forums, courses, and mentorship programs, which can provide valuable insights, support, and guidance throughout the journey.

By the end of Chapter 3, readers have a well-rounded understanding of the factors involved in choosing the right online money-making strategy. They have assessed their interests, skills, market demand, resources, risk tolerance, and long-term goals. Equipped with this knowledge, they are prepared to make informed decisions and move forward with confidence as they delve into the specific strategies detailed in subsequent chapters.

CHAPTER 4: CREATING A WINNING MINDSET FOR ONLINE SUCCESS

The mindset we cultivate plays a vital role in achieving online success. Chapter 4 explores the essential elements of a winning mindset and provides strategies to develop and nurture it. By understanding and harnessing the power of mindset, readers can overcome challenges, stay motivated, and unlock their full potential in the online money-making journey.

4.1 The Power of Mindset: This section highlights the profound impact mindset has on our actions, behaviors, and outcomes. It explains the difference between a fixed mindset, which believes abilities are innate and unchangeable, and a growth mindset, which embraces challenges, values learning, and believes in the potential for growth and improvement. Readers are encouraged to cultivate a growth mindset to unlock their true potential in the online realm.

4.2 Embracing a Positive Attitude: A positive attitude is a cornerstone of a winning mindset. This section explores the power of positivity in overcoming obstacles, bouncing back from failures, and maintaining resilience. It discusses techniques such as gratitude, positive self-talk, visualization, and affirmations that can help readers cultivate and maintain a positive mindset throughout their online money-making journey.

4.3 Setting Clear and Purposeful Goals: Goal setting is crucial for online success, as it provides a clear direction and sense of purpose. This section guides readers in setting SMART (Specific, Measurable, Achievable, Relevant, Time-bound) goals that are aligned with their aspirations. It emphasizes the importance of breaking down big goals into smaller, actionable steps, creating a roadmap for progress and measuring success along the way.

4.4 Overcoming Fear and Self-Doubt: Fear and self-doubt can hinder progress and limit success. This section explores common fears and self-limiting beliefs that may arise in the online money-making journey. It provides strategies to overcome these challenges, such as reframing negative thoughts, building self-confidence through small wins, seeking support from mentors or peers, and embracing failure as a learning opportunity.

4.5 Developing Resilience and Perseverance: Resilience and perseverance are essential qualities for online success, as setbacks and obstacles are inevitable. This section explores strategies to build resilience, such as reframing failures as feedback, adopting a growth mindset, maintaining a support network, and practicing self-care to recharge and maintain emotional well-being. Readers learn to view challenges as opportunities for growth and develop the tenacity to keep pushing forward.

4.6 Continuous Learning and Adaptation: The digital landscape is dynamic, requiring individuals to stay adaptable and continuously learn and evolve. This section emphasizes the importance of embracing a mindset of continuous learning. It explores strategies such as seeking knowledge through courses, books, podcasts, and online communities. Readers are encouraged to stay updated on industry trends, experiment with new strategies, and adapt their approaches based on emerging opportunities.

4.7 Cultivating Discipline and Time Management: Discipline and effective time management are crucial for online success. This section provides insights into cultivating discipline by creating routines, setting priorities, eliminating distractions, and practicing focus and concentration. It explores productivity techniques such as the Pomodoro Technique, time blocking, and task prioritization, enabling readers to optimize their time and productivity in pursuit of their online money-making goals.

4.8 Building a Supportive Network: A supportive network can provide encouragement, guidance, and accountability on the online money-making journey. This section discusses the importance of surrounding oneself with like-minded individuals who share similar goals and aspirations. It explores ways to build a supportive network, such as joining online communities, attending industry events, and seeking mentorship or accountability partnerships.

4.9 Practicing Gratitude and Celebrating Milestones: Gratitude and celebrating milestones are powerful practices that fuel motivation and enhance well-being. This section explores the benefits of gratitude and encourages readers to cultivate a habit of expressing gratitude for progress, opportunities, and achievements. It emphasizes the importance of celebrating milestones, no matter how small, as a means of reinforcing positive momentum and fostering a sense of accomplishment.

By the end of Chapter 4, readers have gained a comprehensive understanding of the essential elements of a winning mindset for online success. They have learned strategies to embrace a growth mindset, develop a positive attitude, set purposeful goals, overcome fear and self-doubt, build resilience, adapt to changes, cultivate discipline, nurture a supportive network, and practice gratitude. Equipped with this powerful mindset, readers are prepared to face the challenges and opportunities of the online money-making journey with confidence and determination.

CHAPTER 5: NICHE SELECTION AND MARKET RESEARCH

Choosing the right niche is a critical step in online money-making. Chapter 5 focuses on the process of niche selection and market research, enabling readers to identify profitable and viable niches within the digital landscape. By understanding the importance of niche selection and mastering effective market research techniques, readers can position themselves strategically to succeed in their online ventures.

5.1 Understanding the Significance of Niche Selection: This section highlights the significance of niche selection in the online money-making journey. It explains that choosing a specific niche allows individuals to target a well-defined audience, differentiate themselves from competitors, and build expertise and credibility. Readers learn that a well-chosen niche increases their chances of success by focusing their efforts and resources on a specific market segment.

5.2 Identifying Personal Interests and Expertise: Niche selection begins with self-reflection and identifying personal interests, passions, and areas of expertise. This section encourages readers to explore their own skills, knowledge, and experiences to find niches that align with their interests. It emphasizes that working in a niche that one enjoys not only provides fulfillment but also enhances motivation and dedication in the long run.

5.3 Assessing Market Demand and Trends: Understanding market demand and trends is crucial in selecting a profitable niche. This section guides readers through effective market research techniques to assess the demand for their chosen niche. It explores tools and resources such as keyword research, trend analysis, industry reports, and social media listening to gather insights on market demand, customer needs, and emerging trends.

5.4 Analyzing Competitor Landscape: Assessing the competitive landscape is an essential aspect of niche selection. This section explains the importance of analyzing competitors within the chosen niche. It explores techniques such as competitor research, SWOT analysis (Strengths, Weaknesses, Opportunities, Threats), and studying competitor websites, content, pricing, and customer feedback. Readers gain insights into competitors' strategies and identify gaps and opportunities for differentiation.

5.5 Defining Target Audience and Buyer Personas: Understanding the target audience is crucial for successful niche selection. This section emphasizes the importance of defining target audience demographics, psychographics, preferences, and pain points. It explores the concept of buyer personas, enabling readers to create detailed profiles of their ideal customers. By understanding their target audience, readers can tailor their products, services, and marketing efforts to meet specific needs.

5.6 Evaluating Monetization Potential: Assessing the monetization potential of a niche is a critical consideration. This section explores different monetization methods such as advertising, affiliate marketing, e-commerce, digital products, services, and subscriptions. Readers learn how to evaluate the profit potential, pricing models, and scalability of their chosen niche, ensuring that it aligns with their financial goals and desired income streams.

5.7 Conducting Keyword Research: Keyword research is a valuable tool in niche selection and SEO (Search Engine Optimization). This section explains the process of conducting keyword research to uncover high-demand and low-competition keywords related to the chosen niche. Readers learn how to use keyword research tools and techniques to optimize their website or content for search engines, enhancing their visibility and attracting relevant organic traffic.

5.8 Testing and Validating the Niche: Before fully committing to a niche, testing and validation are essential steps. This section explores strategies for testing the market response to the chosen niche. It discusses techniques such as creating minimum viable products (MVPs), conducting surveys, gathering feedback, and analyzing conversion rates. By testing the niche's viability, readers can make informed decisions and refine their approach based on real-world feedback.

5.9 Adapting and Evolving with Market Changes: The digital landscape is dynamic, and market trends may change over time. This section emphasizes the need for flexibility and adaptability in niche selection. Readers learn the importance of monitoring market changes, staying updated on industry trends, and being open to pivoting or expanding into related niches when opportunities arise. By embracing change, readers can remain relevant and maximize their chances of long-term success.

By the end of Chapter 5, readers have gained a comprehensive understanding of niche selection and market research. They have learned how to identify personal interests, assess market demand, analyze competition, define target audiences, evaluate monetization potential, conduct keyword research, test and validate their chosen niche, and adapt to market changes. Armed with this knowledge, readers are well-equipped to select a profitable niche and proceed with confidence to the next stages of their online money-making journey.

CHAPTER 6: BUILDING A PERSONAL BRAND ONLINE

In the digital age, building a strong personal brand is a key factor in online success. Chapter 6 focuses on the process of building a personal brand online, enabling readers to establish a distinct and influential presence that resonates with their target audience. By understanding the importance of personal branding and mastering effective strategies, readers can cultivate trust, credibility, and recognition in their chosen niche.

6.1 Understanding the Power of Personal Branding: This section highlights the significance of personal branding in the online realm. It explains that a personal brand is the perception and reputation individuals build around themselves. It explores how personal branding helps differentiate individuals from competitors, establishes credibility, fosters trust, and attracts opportunities. Readers gain an understanding of how a strong personal brand can significantly impact their online money-making journey.

6.2 Defining Your Unique Value Proposition: Defining a unique value proposition is a crucial step in building a personal brand. This section guides readers to identify their unique skills, experiences, perspectives, and qualities that set them apart. It explores the process of crafting a clear and compelling value proposition that communicates the benefits and value individuals bring to their target audience. Readers learn how to articulate their unique selling points effectively.

6.3 Clarifying Your Brand Identity: Brand identity encompasses visual and verbal elements that shape individuals' brand image. This section explores strategies for clarifying brand identity, including choosing a memorable brand name, creating a distinctive logo, defining brand colors, and developing a consistent visual aesthetic. Readers gain insights into creating a brand identity that aligns with their values, niche, and target audience, enabling them to build a recognizable and cohesive brand presence.

6.4 Crafting Your Brand Story: A compelling brand story helps connect individuals with their audience on a deeper level. This section delves into the process of crafting an authentic and engaging brand story that communicates individuals' purpose, values, and journey. It explores storytelling techniques, such as identifying core narratives, using emotional triggers, and highlighting personal experiences that resonate with the audience. Readers learn to captivate and engage their audience through storytelling.

6.5 Establishing Your Online Presence: An online presence is crucial for personal branding. This section guides readers through the process of establishing a strong online presence across various platforms. It explores techniques such as creating a professional website or blog, optimizing social media profiles, utilizing professional networking platforms, and leveraging content marketing strategies. Readers learn to strategically showcase their expertise, share valuable content, and engage with their audience effectively.

6.6 Building an Engaged Social Media Following: Social media platforms provide powerful tools for personal branding. This section explores strategies for building an engaged social media following. It discusses techniques such as identifying relevant social media platforms, creating a content strategy, using storytelling and visual elements, engaging with followers, and leveraging influencers or collaborations. Readers gain insights into nurturing a loyal and active community around their personal brand.

6.7 Consistently Delivering Value: Delivering consistent value is essential for establishing credibility and trust. This section emphasizes the importance of consistently providing valuable content, insights, and expertise to the target audience. It explores techniques such as blogging, vlogging, podcasting, creating digital products, offering free resources or guides, and hosting webinars or live sessions. Readers learn to position themselves as valuable resources and thought leaders within their niche.

6.8 Cultivating Relationships and Networking: Building relationships and networking play a vital role in personal branding. This section explores strategies for cultivating relationships with peers, influencers, industry experts, and potential clients or customers. It discusses techniques such as attending industry events, participating in online communities, collaborating on projects, providing genuine support and engagement, and leveraging partnerships. Readers learn to expand their network and establish valuable connections.

6.9 Monitoring and Managing Your Online Reputation: Maintaining a positive online reputation is crucial for personal branding. This section explores strategies for monitoring and managing online reputation. It discusses techniques such as conducting regular online searches, utilizing online reputation management tools, responding to feedback or reviews professionally, and addressing any negative publicity or misinformation promptly. Readers gain insights into safeguarding and managing their brand reputation effectively.

6.10 Evolving and Growing Your Personal Brand: A personal brand is not static but evolves and grows over time. This section emphasizes the importance of continuous improvement, learning, and adaptation. It explores strategies such as seeking feedback, analyzing data and metrics, staying updated on industry trends, and embracing new opportunities. Readers learn to evolve their personal brand to remain relevant and resonate with their evolving audience.

By the end of Chapter 6, readers have gained a comprehensive

understanding of the process of building a personal brand online. They have learned strategies to define their unique value proposition, clarify their brand identity, craft a compelling brand story, establish an online presence, build an engaged social media following, consistently deliver value, cultivate relationships, monitor and manage their online reputation, and evolve their personal brand over time. Armed with this knowledge, readers are well-prepared to cultivate a powerful personal brand that fuels their online money-making success.

CHAPTER 7: MONETIZING YOUR BLOG OR WEBSITE

In the digital landscape, blogs and websites offer lucrative opportunities for online money-making. Chapter 7 explores the strategies and techniques for monetizing a blog or website effectively. By understanding the various monetization methods, optimizing user experience, and implementing revenue-generating strategies, readers can transform their online platforms into profitable ventures.

7.1 Understanding the Potential of Blog and Website Monetization: This section highlights the potential of monetizing a blog or website. It explores how valuable content, engaged audiences, and targeted traffic can be leveraged to generate revenue. Readers gain an understanding of the different monetization methods available and the factors to consider when selecting the most suitable strategies for their specific blog or website.

7.2 Creating High-Quality and Valuable Content: High-quality and valuable content is the foundation of successful blog or website monetization. This section emphasizes the importance of creating original, engaging, and relevant content that meets the needs and interests of the target audience. It explores techniques such as conducting thorough research, incorporating storytelling, using visuals, and delivering actionable insights. Readers learn to develop content that attracts and retains a loyal audience.

7.3 Optimizing User Experience and Website Design: A positive user experience and an appealing website design are critical for monetization success. This section explores strategies for optimizing user experience, such as ensuring fast loading times, easy navigation, mobile responsiveness, and clear call-to-action elements. It discusses the importance of creating a visually appealing design that aligns with the brand and enhances the overall user experience. Readers gain insights into providing a seamless and enjoyable browsing experience for their audience.

7.4 Implementing Display Advertising: Display advertising is a common monetization method for blogs and websites. This section explores strategies for implementing display advertising, such as using ad networks like Google AdSense, understanding ad placements, and optimizing ad performance. It discusses considerations for balancing user experience and ad revenue, including ad sizes, placements, and the use of ad blockers. Readers gain insights into maximizing the revenue potential of display advertising.

7.5 Exploring Affiliate Marketing: Affiliate marketing offers a powerful opportunity for monetization. This section explores the concept of affiliate marketing, where bloggers or website owners earn a commission for promoting other people's products or services. It discusses strategies for finding relevant affiliate programs, incorporating affiliate links effectively, and building trust with the audience. Readers gain insights into leveraging affiliate marketing to generate revenue through product recommendations and sponsored content.

7.6 Creating and Selling Digital Products: Creating and selling digital products can be a lucrative monetization avenue. This section explores the process of creating digital products such as e-books, online courses, templates, or software. It discusses strategies for developing high-value products, setting competitive pricing, implementing secure payment gateways, and marketing the products effectively. Readers learn how to leverage their expertise and provide value through digital products.

7.7 Generating Revenue with Sponsored Content: Sponsored content provides an opportunity to collaborate with brands and earn revenue. This section explores strategies for working with brands, negotiating partnerships, and creating sponsored content that aligns with the blog or website's niche and audience. It discusses considerations such as transparency, maintaining authenticity, and ensuring sponsored content provides value to the audience. Readers gain insights into monetizing their platform through sponsored collaborations.

7.8 Offering Premium Memberships or Subscriptions: Premium memberships or subscriptions can provide a recurring revenue stream for blogs or websites. This section explores strategies for offering premium content or exclusive access to a dedicated audience segment. It discusses considerations such as determining membership benefits, pricing models, creating gated content, and maintaining member engagement. Readers gain insights into implementing premium memberships or subscriptions to monetize their platform effectively.

7.9 Leveraging Email Marketing for Monetization: Email marketing is a powerful tool for monetization and audience engagement. This section explores strategies for building an email list, creating compelling newsletters, and leveraging email marketing to promote products, services, or affiliate offers. It discusses techniques for segmenting the email list, personalizing content, and nurturing relationships with subscribers. Readers gain insights into maximizing the revenue potential of email marketing.

7.10 Exploring Additional Monetization Methods: This section introduces readers to additional monetization methods that can complement their blog or website. It explores strategies such as sponsored events or webinars, selling merchandise or physical products, offering consulting or coaching services, hosting online courses, or leveraging crowdfunding platforms. Readers gain insights into diversifying their revenue streams and exploring unique opportunities for monetization.

By the end of Chapter 7, readers have gained a comprehensive

understanding of monetizing a blog or website. They have learned strategies to create high-quality content, optimize user experience, implement display advertising, leverage affiliate marketing, create and sell digital products, generate revenue through sponsored content, offer premium memberships or subscriptions, utilize email marketing, and explore additional monetization methods. Equipped with this knowledge, readers can strategically monetize their blog or website and maximize their online money-making potential.

CHAPTER 8: MASTERING AFFILIATE MARKETING

Affiliate marketing is a powerful online money-making strategy that allows individuals to earn commissions by promoting other people's products or services. Chapter 8 delves into the intricacies of affiliate marketing, equipping readers with the knowledge and strategies to master this lucrative technique. By understanding the affiliate marketing ecosystem, building effective partnerships, optimizing promotions, and maximizing conversions, readers can leverage affiliate marketing to generate significant income.

8.1 Understanding the Fundamentals of Affiliate Marketing: This section provides an overview of affiliate marketing, explaining its core principles and the roles of key players. It explores the affiliate marketing ecosystem, which includes merchants or advertisers, affiliate networks, and affiliate marketers. Readers gain a clear understanding of how affiliate marketing works and the opportunities it presents for generating revenue.

8.2 Selecting Profitable Affiliate Programs: Choosing the right affiliate programs is crucial for success in affiliate marketing. This section guides readers through the process of selecting profitable affiliate programs that align with their niche and target audience. It explores factors to consider, such as commission rates, product quality, affiliate support, payment terms, and tracking and reporting capabilities. Readers learn strategies to identify reputable and high-converting affiliate programs.

8.3 Building Strong Relationships with Merchants: Building strong relationships with merchants is essential in affiliate marketing. This section discusses strategies for establishing trust and credibility with merchants. It explores techniques such as reaching out to merchants, demonstrating value through audience insights, negotiating favorable commission rates, and maintaining open communication channels. Readers gain insights into fostering collaborative partnerships that benefit both parties.

8.4 Developing an Affiliate Marketing Strategy: A well-defined affiliate marketing strategy sets the foundation for success. This section explores the process of developing an effective strategy. It covers aspects such as defining target audiences, selecting suitable products or services to promote, setting promotional goals, creating a content calendar, and utilizing various marketing channels. Readers learn to align their affiliate marketing efforts with their overall business objectives.

8.5 Creating Compelling Affiliate Content: Compelling content is the key to attracting and engaging audiences in affiliate marketing. This section explores strategies for creating high-quality affiliate content that educates, informs, and persuades. It discusses techniques such as writing product reviews, crafting informative blog posts, producing engaging videos, utilizing persuasive storytelling, and incorporating visual elements. Readers gain insights into creating content that resonates with their audience and drives conversions.

8.6 Leveraging SEO for Affiliate Marketing: Search Engine Optimization (SEO) plays a crucial role in driving organic traffic and enhancing visibility in affiliate marketing. This section explains the principles of SEO and explores strategies for optimizing affiliate content for search engines. It covers techniques such as keyword research, on-page optimization, link building, and optimizing website speed and mobile responsiveness. Readers learn to increase their chances of ranking higher in search engine results, driving targeted traffic to their affiliate promotions.

8.7 Harnessing the Power of Social Media: Social media platforms provide immense opportunities for affiliate marketing. This section explores strategies for leveraging social media to promote affiliate products or services effectively. It covers techniques such as creating engaging social media posts, utilizing influencers or brand ambassadors, participating in relevant communities or groups, and running targeted ad campaigns. Readers gain insights into maximizing their reach, engagement, and conversions through social media channels.

8.8 Implementing Email Marketing for Affiliate Promotions: Email marketing is a powerful tool for nurturing relationships and driving affiliate conversions. This section discusses strategies for implementing email marketing in affiliate promotions. It explores techniques such as building an email list, segmenting subscribers, creating compelling newsletters or campaigns, using personalized recommendations, and incorporating persuasive call-to-action elements. Readers learn to effectively leverage email marketing to drive affiliate sales and build long-term relationships with subscribers.

8.9 Tracking and Analyzing Affiliate Performance: Tracking and analyzing affiliate performance is crucial for optimizing campaigns and maximizing conversions. This section explores techniques for tracking affiliate links, monitoring clicks, conversions, and revenue generated. It discusses the use of affiliate tracking platforms and analytics tools to gain insights into campaign performance, identify top-performing products or promotions, and make data-driven optimizations. Readers gain the ability to evaluate the effectiveness of their affiliate marketing efforts and refine their strategies accordingly.

8.10 Scaling and Expanding Affiliate Marketing Efforts: Scaling and expanding affiliate marketing efforts can lead to increased revenue and business growth. This section explores strategies for scaling affiliate marketing, such as diversifying product promotions, expanding to new niches or markets, leveraging automation tools, and exploring advanced techniques like multi-tier affiliate marketing or joint ventures. Readers gain insights into maximizing their earning potential and expanding their affiliate marketing business.

By the end of Chapter 8, readers have gained a comprehensive understanding of affiliate marketing. They have learned strategies to select profitable affiliate programs, build strong merchant relationships, develop effective affiliate marketing strategies, create compelling content, leverage SEO and social media, implement email marketing, track and analyze performance, and scale their affiliate marketing efforts. Armed with this knowledge, readers are well-prepared to master affiliate marketing and unlock its potential for significant online money-making success.

CHAPTER 9: CREATING AND SELLING INFORMATION PRODUCTS

Creating and selling information products is a popular and profitable online money-making strategy. Chapter 9 explores the process of creating and selling information products, enabling readers to leverage their knowledge and expertise to generate revenue. By understanding the different types of information products, developing compelling content, designing effective sales funnels, and implementing marketing strategies, readers can create and sell successful information products.

9.1 Understanding Information Products: This section provides an overview of information products and their potential for generating income. It explains that information products are digital or downloadable resources that provide valuable knowledge, insights, or solutions to a specific target audience. It explores various types of information products, including e-books, online courses, webinars, video tutorials, templates, and membership sites. Readers gain an understanding of the diverse range of information products they can create and sell.

9.2 Identifying Profitable Information Product Ideas: Identifying profitable information product ideas is crucial for success. This section guides readers through the process of identifying market demand, conducting niche research, and validating information product ideas. It explores techniques such as keyword research, competitor analysis, surveys, and audience feedback. Readers learn strategies to identify information product ideas that align with their expertise and cater to the needs of their target audience.

9.3 Developing Compelling Content: Compelling content is the cornerstone of successful information products. This section explores strategies for developing high-quality and engaging content. It covers aspects such as structuring the content, organizing information effectively, incorporating storytelling techniques, using visuals and multimedia elements, and ensuring clarity and coherence. Readers gain insights into creating content that educates, entertains, and adds value to their target audience.

9.4 Designing Effective Sales Funnels: Sales funnels play a crucial role in driving conversions and maximizing sales of information products. This section delves into the process of designing effective sales funnels. It explores techniques such as creating lead magnets to capture email addresses, developing sales pages or landing pages, implementing upsells and downsells, and optimizing checkout processes. Readers learn to design sales funnels that guide potential customers through the purchasing journey.

9.5 Crafting Irresistible Sales Copy: Compelling sales copy is essential for persuading potential customers to purchase information products. This section discusses strategies for crafting persuasive and irresistible sales copy. It explores techniques such as writing compelling headlines, emphasizing benefits, addressing objections, incorporating social proof, and utilizing persuasive storytelling. Readers gain insights into creating sales copy that captivates their target audience and compels them to take action.

9.6 Creating High-Quality Visuals and Design: Visuals and design play a crucial role in enhancing the appeal and professionalism of information products. This section explores strategies for creating high-quality visuals and design elements. It covers aspects such as selecting appropriate colors, fonts, and graphics, creating engaging cover designs, and formatting content for readability. Readers gain insights into creating visually appealing information products that enhance the user experience.

9.7 Implementing Secure Payment and Delivery Systems: Implementing secure payment and delivery systems is crucial for a seamless customer experience. This section discusses strategies for selecting and integrating payment gateways, ensuring secure transactions, and delivering information products to customers efficiently. It explores tools and platforms that facilitate payment processing, digital product delivery, and customer support. Readers gain insights into providing a secure and user-friendly purchasing process.

9.8 Pricing and Packaging Information Products: Determining the pricing and packaging of information products requires careful consideration. This section explores strategies for pricing information products based on factors such as market demand, perceived value, competition, and production costs. It discusses pricing models, such as one-time purchases, subscriptions, or tiered pricing. Readers learn techniques to package their information products in a way that appeals to their target audience and maximizes profitability.

9.9 Implementing Marketing and Promotion Strategies: Effective marketing and promotion strategies are essential for driving awareness and sales of information products. This section explores strategies for marketing and promoting information products. It covers techniques such as content marketing, email marketing, social media marketing, influencer partnerships, affiliate marketing, paid advertising, and search engine optimization. Readers gain insights into implementing a comprehensive marketing plan to reach their target audience and generate sales.

9.10 Providing Ongoing Support and Updates: Providing ongoing support and updates is crucial for customer satisfaction and retention. This section discusses strategies for offering customer support, addressing inquiries or issues, and providing regular updates to information products. It explores techniques such as creating customer support channels, offering a knowledge base or FAQ section, and implementing a system for product updates or revisions. Readers gain insights into fostering positive customer experiences and building long-term relationships.

By the end of Chapter 9, readers have gained a comprehensive understanding of creating and selling information products. They have learned strategies to identify profitable product ideas, develop compelling content, design effective sales funnels, craft persuasive sales copy, create high-quality visuals, implement secure payment and delivery systems, determine pricing and packaging, implement marketing and promotion strategies, and provide ongoing support. Armed with this knowledge, readers can create and sell information products that resonate with their target audience and generate significant online revenue.

CHAPTER 10: LAUNCHING AND SCALING AN E-COMMERCE STORE

Launching and scaling an e-commerce store is an exciting and potentially lucrative venture in the online money-making landscape. Chapter 10 delves into the intricacies of establishing and growing a successful e-commerce store, providing readers with the knowledge and strategies to navigate the competitive e-commerce market. By understanding the key elements of a successful e-commerce business, selecting the right products, optimizing the user experience, implementing effective marketing tactics, and scaling operations, readers can create a thriving online store.

10.1 Understanding the E-commerce Landscape: This section provides an overview of the e-commerce landscape and its vast potential for generating revenue. It explores the growth of online shopping, emerging trends, and the importance of establishing a strong online presence. Readers gain an understanding of the opportunities and challenges presented by the e-commerce market, setting the stage for launching their own e-commerce store.

10.2 Defining Your E-commerce Business Model: Defining a clear and effective e-commerce business model is crucial for success. This section explores different business models such as dropshipping, inventory-based, print-on-demand, subscription-based, or multi-vendor marketplaces. It discusses the advantages, challenges, and revenue potential of each model, helping readers choose the most suitable one for their goals and resources.

10.3 Selecting Profitable Products to Sell: Selecting profitable products is a critical aspect of launching an e-commerce store. This section guides readers through the process of product selection, considering factors such as market demand, competition, profit margins, and target audience preferences. It explores techniques such as conducting market research, analyzing trends, leveraging keyword tools, and evaluating supplier options. Readers gain insights into identifying winning products that align with their niche and target market.

10.4 Building a User-Friendly Website: A user-friendly website is essential for engaging customers and driving conversions in e-commerce. This section explores strategies for building an effective e-commerce website. It covers aspects such as choosing a reliable e-commerce platform, designing an intuitive layout, optimizing product pages for search engines, ensuring mobile responsiveness, implementing secure payment gateways, and enhancing the overall user experience. Readers gain insights into creating a website that instills trust, facilitates seamless navigation, and encourages purchases.

10.5 Optimizing Product Listings and Descriptions: Optimizing product listings and descriptions is crucial for driving traffic and sales. This section explores strategies for creating compelling product descriptions that resonate with the target audience. It covers techniques such as incorporating relevant keywords, highlighting product features and benefits, using persuasive language, and including high-quality product images. Readers gain insights into optimizing their product listings to attract and convert potential customers.

10.6 Implementing Effective Marketing Tactics: Effective marketing tactics are key to driving traffic and sales in an e-commerce store. This section explores strategies for implementing various marketing channels and techniques. It covers aspects such as content marketing, search engine optimization (SEO), social media marketing, email marketing, influencer partnerships, paid advertising, and affiliate marketing. Readers gain insights into developing a comprehensive marketing plan tailored to their target audience and budget.

10.7 Enhancing Customer Experience and Support: Providing exceptional customer experience and support is crucial for e-commerce success. This section explores strategies for enhancing the customer journey, including aspects such as responsive customer support, easy returns and refunds, personalized recommendations, loyalty programs, and user-generated reviews and testimonials. Readers gain insights into fostering positive customer relationships and building brand loyalty in their e-commerce store.

10.8 Implementing Inventory and Order Management Systems: Efficient inventory and order management are essential for smooth operations in an e-commerce store. This section discusses strategies for implementing inventory management systems, tracking stock levels, automating order fulfillment, and optimizing shipping and logistics. It explores tools and techniques that enable readers to streamline their inventory and order processes, reducing errors and ensuring timely deliveries.

10.9 Analyzing and Optimizing Store Performance: Analyzing and optimizing store performance is crucial for ongoing success. This section explores strategies for tracking and analyzing key performance metrics, such as conversion rates, average order value, customer lifetime value, and customer acquisition costs. It discusses techniques such as using analytics tools, conducting A/B testing, implementing conversion rate optimization strategies, and leveraging customer feedback. Readers gain insights into making data-driven decisions and continuously improving their e-commerce store's performance.

10.10 Scaling and Expanding Your E-commerce Business: Scaling and expanding an e-commerce business is the ultimate goal for long-term success. This section explores strategies for scaling operations, increasing product offerings, expanding into new markets or platforms, and exploring partnerships or collaborations. It discusses considerations such as hiring additional staff, optimizing supply chain management, diversifying revenue streams, and utilizing automation and technology. Readers gain insights into planning for growth and seizing opportunities for expansion.

By the end of Chapter 10, readers have gained a comprehensive understanding of launching and scaling an e-commerce store. They have learned strategies to define their business model, select profitable products, build a user-friendly website, optimize product listings, implement effective marketing tactics, enhance customer experience and support, implement inventory and order management systems, analyze and optimize business performance, and navigate the challenges of logistics and fulfillment. Additionally, readers have explored various methods to drive traffic to their e-commerce store, including search engine optimization (SEO), social media marketing, and paid advertising campaigns. They have also delved into the world of data analytics, understanding how to track and measure key performance indicators (KPIs) to make informed business decisions. Furthermore, readers have gained insights into the importance of building a strong brand identity and establishing trust with customers through consistent messaging and excellent customer service.

CHAPTER 11: EXPLORING DROPSHIPPING AND PRINT ON DEMAND

Dropshipping and print on demand are two popular business models in the e-commerce industry that offer entrepreneurs the opportunity to start and run their own online stores without the need for inventory management or upfront product investments. Chapter 11 delves into the details of dropshipping and print on demand, providing readers with an in-depth understanding of these business models, their advantages and challenges, and the steps involved in setting up and running a successful venture.

11.1 Understanding Dropshipping: Dropshipping is a business model where entrepreneurs act as intermediaries between customers and suppliers. This section explains the fundamentals of dropshipping, including how it works and the key players involved—retailers, suppliers, and customers. Readers gain insights into the advantages of dropshipping, such as low startup costs, flexibility, and the ability to offer a wide range of products without the need for inventory storage.

11.2 The Dropshipping Process: This section walks readers through the dropshipping process, step by step. It covers aspects such as selecting a niche, sourcing reliable suppliers, setting up an e-commerce platform, importing product listings, managing orders, and handling customer support. Readers gain a comprehensive understanding of how each stage of the dropshipping process works, ensuring they are well-equipped to navigate the operational aspects of their dropshipping business.

11.3 Finding Reliable Dropshipping Suppliers: Finding reliable dropshipping suppliers is crucial for a successful dropshipping business. This section explores strategies for sourcing reputable suppliers, including conducting thorough research, leveraging supplier directories, attending trade shows, and reaching out to manufacturers or wholesalers. It discusses considerations such as product quality, pricing, shipping options, inventory availability, and supplier communication. Readers gain insights into building strong relationships with reliable suppliers.

11.4 Setting Up an E-commerce Platform for Dropshipping: Setting up an e-commerce platform is a key step in launching a dropshipping business. This section explores different e-commerce platform options, such as Shopify, WooCommerce, or Magento, and guides readers through the process of selecting and configuring the platform that best suits their needs. It covers aspects such as choosing a domain name, designing a user-friendly website, integrating payment gateways, and optimizing the platform for conversions. Readers gain insights into creating an effective online store for their dropshipping business.

11.5 Importing and Managing Product Listings: Importing and managing product listings efficiently is crucial for a streamlined dropshipping operation. This section discusses strategies for importing product listings from suppliers to the e-commerce platform, optimizing product titles and descriptions for search engines, and managing product inventory and pricing updates. It explores tools and techniques that automate the listing and inventory management process, ensuring accurate and up-to-date product information. Readers gain insights into maintaining a well-organized and competitive product catalog.

11.6 Handling Orders and Shipping: Efficient order management and shipping processes are essential in dropshipping. This section guides readers through strategies for managing and fulfilling customer orders seamlessly. It covers aspects such as order processing, communicating with suppliers, tracking shipments, handling returns or exchanges, and ensuring customer satisfaction. Readers gain insights into implementing systems and processes that enable smooth order fulfillment and timely delivery.

11.7 Customer Service and Support in Dropshipping: Providing exceptional customer service and support is critical for building trust and loyalty in a dropshipping business. This section explores strategies for delivering top-notch customer service, including establishing communication channels, responding to inquiries promptly, handling customer complaints or issues, and providing clear and accurate product information. Readers gain insights into nurturing positive customer relationships and ensuring a positive shopping experience.

11.8 Understanding Print on Demand: Print on demand (POD) is a business model that allows entrepreneurs to sell custom-designed or personalized products without the need for inventory or upfront production costs. This section explains the concept of print on demand and its advantages, such as low startup costs, the ability to offer unique and customized products, and the flexibility to experiment with different designs and niches. Readers gain insights into the potential of print on demand in the e-commerce industry.

11.9 Creating and Selling Custom Products: Creating and selling custom products is a central aspect of the print on demand business model. This section explores strategies for designing and sourcing custom products, including apparel, accessories, home decor, or promotional items. It discusses techniques for creating compelling designs, utilizing design software or hiring designers, selecting quality products, and integrating the print on demand production process. Readers gain insights into developing a diverse and appealing product catalog.

11.10 Partnering with Print on Demand Platforms: Partnering with print on demand platforms is a crucial step in launching a print on demand business. This section discusses popular print on demand platforms, such as Printful, Printify, or Redbubble, and guides readers through the process of selecting and integrating a platform that aligns with their business goals. It explores aspects such as product selection, design uploading, pricing, branding options, and fulfillment and shipping processes. Readers gain insights into leveraging print on demand platforms to streamline production and delivery.

11.11 Marketing and Promoting Dropshipping and Print on Demand Products: Marketing and promotion are vital for attracting customers and driving sales in dropshipping and print on demand businesses. This section explores strategies for marketing and promoting products, including content marketing, social media advertising, influencer partnerships, email marketing, search engine optimization, and paid advertising. It discusses techniques for targeting the right audience, creating compelling product descriptions, and leveraging visual content. Readers gain insights into developing a comprehensive marketing strategy for their dropshipping or print on demand business.

11.12 Scaling and Expanding Dropshipping and Print on Demand Ventures: Scaling and expanding dropshipping and print on demand ventures is the ultimate goal for business growth. This section explores strategies for scaling operations, diversifying product offerings, expanding into new markets, or exploring additional business models. It discusses considerations such as outsourcing tasks, automating processes, leveraging data and analytics, and exploring new product niches or target audiences. Readers gain insights into planning for growth and optimizing their dropshipping or print on demand business for long-term success.

By the end of Chapter 11, readers have gained a comprehensive understanding of dropshipping and print on demand business models. They have learned the intricacies of sourcing reliable suppliers, setting up e-commerce platforms, managing product listings, handling orders and shipping, providing excellent customer service, creating and selling custom products, partnering with print on demand platforms, marketing and promoting products effectively, and scaling their dropshipping or print on demand ventures. Armed with this knowledge, readers can embark on their entrepreneurial journey and build successful and profitable e-commerce businesses.

CHAPTER 12: UNLOCKING THE POWER OF SOCIAL MEDIA MARKETING

Social media has transformed the way businesses connect with their target audience and promote their products or services. Chapter 12 delves into the world of social media marketing, equipping readers with the knowledge and strategies to harness the power of social media platforms to drive brand awareness, engage with customers, and generate revenue. By understanding the different social media platforms, developing an effective social media strategy, creating engaging content, utilizing advertising tools, and analyzing performance metrics, readers can unlock the potential of social media marketing for their business.

12.1 Understanding the Impact of Social Media Marketing: This section explores the profound impact of social media marketing on businesses of all sizes. It discusses the benefits of social media marketing, such as increased brand visibility, improved customer engagement, enhanced customer relationships, and expanded reach. Readers gain insights into the vast potential of social media platforms as powerful marketing tools.

12.2 Choosing the Right Social Media Platforms: Choosing the right social media platforms is essential to reach the target audience effectively. This section provides an overview of popular social media platforms, such as Facebook, Instagram, Twitter, LinkedIn, YouTube, and Pinterest. It explores the demographics and features of each platform, helping readers identify the platforms that align with their target audience and marketing objectives. Readers gain insights into making informed decisions about which social media platforms to focus on.

12.3 Developing a Social Media Strategy: A well-defined social media strategy sets the foundation for success. This section explores the process of developing a comprehensive social media strategy. It covers aspects such as defining goals and objectives, identifying target audience personas, conducting competitor analysis, establishing a unique brand voice and tone, and determining key performance indicators (KPIs) to measure success. Readers gain insights into creating a tailored social media strategy that aligns with their business objectives.

12.4 Creating Engaging Social Media Content: Engaging content is at the core of successful social media marketing. This section discusses strategies for creating compelling content that resonates with the target audience. It explores techniques such as storytelling, visual elements, user-generated content, interactive posts, and behind-the-scenes glimpses. Readers gain insights into crafting engaging social media content that grabs attention, sparks conversation, and encourages sharing.

12.5 Utilizing Social Media Advertising: Social media advertising offers targeted and cost-effective opportunities to reach a wider audience. This section explores strategies for utilizing social media advertising tools, such as Facebook Ads, Instagram Ads, or LinkedIn Ads. It covers aspects such as audience targeting, ad formats, budgeting, and ad optimization techniques. Readers gain insights into leveraging social media advertising to maximize their reach and drive conversions.

12.6 Growing and Engaging a Social Media Following: Building a loyal and engaged social media following is vital for success. This section discusses strategies for growing and engaging a social media following organically. It explores techniques such as optimizing profiles, using hashtags effectively, fostering community engagement, running contests or giveaways, collaborating with influencers, and encouraging user-generated content. Readers gain insights into nurturing a thriving social media community that actively interacts with their brand.

12.7 Leveraging Influencer Marketing: Influencer marketing can amplify brand reach and credibility. This section explores strategies for leveraging influencer marketing on social media platforms. It covers aspects such as identifying relevant influencers, establishing partnerships, creating authentic collaborations, and measuring the effectiveness of influencer campaigns. Readers gain insights into harnessing the power of influencers to reach a wider audience and build trust with their target market.

12.8 Implementing Social Media Customer Service: Social media platforms have become key channels for customer service. This section discusses strategies for implementing effective social media customer service, including timely response management, addressing customer inquiries or complaints, providing solutions publicly or privately, and maintaining a positive brand image. Readers gain insights into delivering exceptional customer service experiences that enhance brand reputation and customer loyalty.

12.9 Analyzing Social Media Metrics and Insights: Analyzing social media metrics and insights is crucial for optimizing performance and measuring the success of social media marketing efforts. This section explores key metrics and analytics tools available on various social media platforms. It covers aspects such as reach, engagement, click-through rates, conversion tracking, and audience demographics. Readers gain insights into leveraging data and analytics to make data-driven decisions and refine their social media strategies.

12.10 Staying Ahead with Social Media Trends: Staying ahead of social media trends is essential to remain competitive. This section explores emerging social media trends and innovations, such as live video streaming, ephemeral content, augmented reality (AR), influencer collaborations, and user-generated content campaigns. Readers gain insights into adapting to evolving social media trends, experimenting with new features, and staying connected with their target audience.

12.11 Managing Social Media Crisis and Reputation: Managing social media crisis and reputation is crucial for brand protection. This section discusses strategies for handling social media crises, including developing crisis response plans, addressing negative feedback or reviews, and managing public relations effectively. It explores techniques for resolving conflicts, offering apologies or solutions, and rebuilding trust. Readers gain insights into safeguarding their brand reputation and mitigating potential risks on social media platforms.

12.12 Scaling and Expanding Social Media Marketing Efforts: Scaling and expanding social media marketing efforts can lead to increased brand visibility and revenue growth. This section explores strategies for scaling social media marketing, such as leveraging automation tools, exploring advanced advertising features, diversifying content formats, and expanding into new social media platforms or markets. Readers gain insights into planning for growth and maximizing the potential of social media marketing.

By the end of Chapter 12, readers have gained a comprehensive understanding of social media marketing. They have learned strategies to choose the right social media platforms, develop an effective social media strategy, create engaging content, utilize social media advertising, grow and engage a social media following, leverage influencer marketing, implement social media customer service, analyze metrics and insights, stay ahead with social media trends, manage crises and reputation, and scale their social media marketing efforts. Armed with this knowledge, readers can leverage the power of social media marketing to drive brand awareness, engage with their target audience, and achieve their business objectives.

CHAPTER 13: HARNESSING THE POTENTIAL OF INFLUENCER MARKETING

Influencer marketing has emerged as a powerful strategy for businesses to connect with their target audience, build brand awareness, and drive conversions. Chapter 13 explores the potential of influencer marketing, providing readers with a comprehensive understanding of this dynamic marketing approach. By understanding the role of influencers, identifying the right influencers for their brand, developing effective influencer partnerships, and measuring campaign success, readers can harness the potential of influencer marketing to propel their business forward.

13.1 Understanding Influencer Marketing: This section provides an overview of influencer marketing and its significance in the modern digital landscape. It explains how influencers, individuals with a dedicated following and influence within a specific niche, can impact consumer behavior and shape brand perceptions. Readers gain insights into the key principles of influencer marketing and its potential to drive brand engagement and sales.

13.2 The Role of Influencers: Understanding the role of influencers is crucial for successful influencer marketing campaigns. This section delves into the different types of influencers, such as macro-influencers, micro-influencers, and nano-influencers, and explores their characteristics, audience reach, and engagement levels. It discusses the benefits and considerations associated with each type, enabling readers to identify the most suitable influencers for their brand objectives.

13.3 Identifying the Right Influencers for Your Brand:

Identifying the right influencers for your brand is a critical step in influencer marketing. This section explores strategies for finding influencers who align with your brand values, target audience, and marketing objectives. It covers techniques such as conducting research, utilizing influencer discovery tools, analyzing audience demographics and engagement metrics, and considering the influencer's content quality and authenticity. Readers gain insights into selecting influencers who can effectively represent and promote their brand.

13.4 Building Authentic Influencer Partnerships: Building authentic and mutually beneficial partnerships with influencers is key to successful influencer marketing campaigns. This section discusses strategies for approaching influencers, establishing relationships, and developing partnership agreements. It explores techniques such as personalized outreach, offering value to influencers, setting clear expectations, and fostering long-term collaborations. Readers gain insights into creating meaningful connections with influencers that result in impactful marketing campaigns.

13.5 Developing Effective Influencer Marketing Campaigns: Developing effective influencer marketing campaigns requires careful planning and execution. This section explores the process of creating impactful campaigns that align with your brand and resonate with the target audience. It covers aspects such as campaign goals and objectives, defining key messages, outlining deliverables and timelines, and providing creative direction to influencers. Readers gain insights into developing compelling influencer marketing campaigns that drive engagement and conversions.

13.6 Crafting Authentic Influencer Content: Authentic content is at the heart of successful influencer marketing campaigns. This section discusses strategies for working with influencers to craft authentic and engaging content that aligns with your brand values and resonates with their audience. It explores techniques such as providing creative freedom to influencers, integrating brand messaging organically, leveraging storytelling, and incorporating user-generated content. Readers gain insights into creating impactful influencer content that sparks interest and drives action.

13.7 Leveraging Different Social Media Platforms: Influencer marketing extends across various social media platforms. This section explores strategies for leveraging different platforms, such as Instagram, YouTube, TikTok, or Twitter, for influencer marketing campaigns. It discusses the unique features and audience demographics of each platform, enabling readers to choose the platforms that align with their target audience and campaign goals. Readers gain insights into adapting influencer marketing strategies to different social media platforms.

13.8 Measuring Influencer Marketing Success: Measuring the success of influencer marketing campaigns is essential for assessing ROI and optimizing future campaigns. This section explores key performance indicators (KPIs) and metrics to track, such as reach, engagement, click-through rates, conversions, and return on ad spend. It discusses tools and techniques for monitoring campaign performance and conducting post-campaign analysis. Readers gain insights into measuring the impact of influencer marketing on their brand's visibility, engagement, and revenue.

13.9 Complying with Influencer Marketing Guidelines: Compliance with influencer marketing guidelines and regulations is crucial to maintain ethical and transparent practices. This section discusses guidelines set by regulatory bodies, such as the Federal Trade Commission (FTC), regarding disclosure of sponsored content, endorsements, and brand partnerships. It explores strategies for ensuring compliance, such as using appropriate disclosure language and working with influencers who adhere to ethical practices. Readers gain insights into navigating legal and ethical considerations in influencer marketing.

13.10 Building Long-Term Relationships with Influencers: Building long-term relationships with influencers can yield ongoing benefits for your brand. This section discusses strategies for nurturing relationships, fostering trust, and incentivizing influencers to maintain long-term partnerships. It explores techniques such as offering exclusivity, providing continuous support, recognizing and rewarding influencers' efforts, and engaging them in brand campaigns beyond one-off collaborations. Readers gain insights into building enduring relationships with influencers that drive sustained brand advocacy.

13.11 Collaborating with Influencers for Product Launches: Influencers can play a pivotal role in product launches, generating buzz and driving sales. This section explores strategies for collaborating with influencers during product launches. It covers aspects such as pre-launch teasers, exclusive sneak peeks, influencer-generated content showcasing the product, and live product demonstrations. Readers gain insights into leveraging the reach and influence of influencers to create excitement and anticipation around new products, ultimately leading to successful launches.

13.12 Managing Influencer Relationships and Campaigns: Effective management of influencer relationships and campaigns is essential for smooth execution and desired outcomes. This section discusses strategies for managing influencer relationships, establishing clear communication channels, setting expectations, providing timely feedback, and ensuring campaign deliverables are met. It explores techniques for streamlining campaign workflows, tracking influencer performance, and optimizing collaborations. Readers gain insights into maintaining strong and productive relationships with influencers throughout their marketing campaigns.

13.13 Integrating Influencer Marketing with Other Marketing Channels: Integrating influencer marketing with other marketing channels can enhance brand visibility and reach.

This section explores strategies for synergizing influencer marketing efforts with other channels, such as content marketing, social media advertising, email marketing, or public relations. It discusses techniques for cross-promoting influencer content, leveraging influencer collaborations in other marketing initiatives, and amplifying campaign messaging through various channels. Readers gain insights into creating cohesive and integrated marketing campaigns that maximize the impact of influencer partnerships.

13.14 Navigating Challenges in Influencer Marketing: Influencer marketing comes with its own set of challenges that need to be navigated effectively. This section discusses common challenges in influencer marketing, such as fake followers, influencer credibility, measurement and attribution, influencer-brand misalignment, and maintaining authenticity. It explores strategies for mitigating these challenges, including vetting influencers, using analytics tools to validate audience engagement, setting clear campaign objectives, and establishing transparent communication with influencers. Readers gain insights into proactively addressing challenges and ensuring successful influencer marketing campaigns.

13.15 Emerging Trends in Influencer Marketing: Influencer marketing continues to evolve with the ever-changing digital landscape. This section explores emerging trends and innovations in influencer marketing. It discusses trends such as the rise of micro-influencers, influencer-generated content, long-form storytelling, live video collaborations, virtual influencer partnerships, and authenticity-focused campaigns. Readers gain insights into staying updated with the latest trends and leveraging them to create impactful influencer marketing strategies.

By the end of Chapter 13, readers have gained a comprehensive understanding of influencer marketing. They have learned the role of influencers, strategies for identifying the right influencers, developing authentic partnerships, crafting engaging content, leveraging different social media platforms, measuring campaign success, complying with guidelines, building long-term relationships, collaborating for product launches, managing influencer relationships and campaigns, integrating with other marketing channels, navigating challenges, and staying informed about emerging trends. Armed with this knowledge, readers can harness the potential of influencer marketing to connect with their target audience, amplify their brand, and achieve their marketing goals.

CHAPTER 14: LEVERAGING YOUTUBE FOR PROFIT

YouTube has emerged as a powerhouse platform for content creation, entertainment, and online marketing. Chapter 14 dives into the world of YouTube and explores how businesses can leverage this platform to generate profits. By understanding the benefits of YouTube marketing, creating a successful YouTube channel, optimizing content for visibility, monetizing videos, engaging with the audience, and analyzing performance metrics, readers can harness the potential of YouTube to drive brand growth and generate revenue.

14.1 The Power of YouTube Marketing: This section highlights the power of YouTube as a marketing platform. It explores the vast audience reach, engagement, and consumption patterns on YouTube, emphasizing the opportunities it presents for businesses to connect with their target audience and promote their products or services. Readers gain insights into the benefits of YouTube marketing, including brand exposure, increased website traffic, lead generation, and enhanced customer engagement.

14.2 Creating a Successful YouTube Channel: Creating a successful YouTube channel is the first step towards leveraging YouTube for profit. This section guides readers through the process of setting up and optimizing a YouTube channel. It covers aspects such as choosing a channel name, designing channel art and thumbnails, writing compelling channel descriptions, and organizing content into playlists. Readers gain insights into creating a visually appealing and user-friendly channel that reflects their brand identity.

14.3 Defining Your YouTube Content Strategy: Defining a

content strategy is essential for consistently delivering valuable and engaging content to the YouTube audience. This section explores strategies for defining a YouTube content strategy, including identifying target audience personas, conducting keyword research, brainstorming content ideas, and creating a content calendar. It discusses the importance of providing educational, entertaining, or inspirational content that aligns with the audience's interests and needs.

14.4 Creating High-Quality Video Content: High-quality video content is crucial for capturing and retaining viewers' attention on YouTube. This section discusses strategies for creating engaging and visually appealing video content. It covers aspects such as scripting, filming techniques, editing, incorporating visuals and graphics, optimizing video length, and using appropriate music or sound effects. Readers gain insights into creating videos that stand out, deliver value, and leave a lasting impression on the audience.

14.5 Optimizing YouTube Videos for Visibility: Optimizing YouTube videos for visibility is key to attracting a wider audience and gaining exposure on the platform. This section explores strategies for optimizing videos for search engine discoverability and suggested video recommendations. It covers techniques such as conducting keyword research, optimizing video titles, descriptions, and tags, utilizing closed captions, adding relevant end screens and cards, and engaging with comments and video responses. Readers gain insights into improving their videos' visibility and increasing their chances of appearing in search results and recommendations.

14.6 Monetizing YouTube Videos: Monetizing YouTube videos enables content creators to generate revenue from their channel. This section discusses strategies for monetizing YouTube videos through the YouTube Partner Program (YPP) and other revenue streams. It covers aspects such as eligibility requirements, enabling monetization features, understanding ad formats, exploring channel memberships, utilizing Super Chat and

Super Stickers, and leveraging sponsored content opportunities. Readers gain insights into generating income through their YouTube channel and diversifying revenue streams.

14.7 Engaging with the YouTube Community: Building an engaged YouTube community is crucial for long-term success on the platform. This section explores strategies for engaging with the YouTube community and fostering meaningful connections with viewers. It covers techniques such as responding to comments, encouraging likes and shares, running contests or giveaways, collaborating with other YouTubers, and hosting live streams or Q&A sessions. Readers gain insights into nurturing a loyal and active community that contributes to the growth and success of their channel.

14.8 Promoting YouTube Videos: Promoting YouTube videos beyond the platform itself can increase visibility and attract a broader audience. This section discusses strategies for promoting YouTube videos through various marketing channels. It explores techniques such as sharing videos on social media, embedding videos on websites or blogs, utilizing email marketing, collaborating with influencers, and leveraging cross-promotion with other content creators. Readers gain insights into expanding the reach of their YouTube videos and driving more traffic to their channel.

14.9 Analyzing YouTube Analytics: Analyzing YouTube analytics provides valuable insights into video performance, audience behavior, and channel growth. This section explores key metrics and features available in YouTube analytics. It covers aspects such as views, watch time, audience retention, demographics, traffic sources, and engagement metrics. Readers gain insights into understanding their audience's preferences, identifying trends, and making data-driven decisions to optimize their content and channel strategy.

14.10 Collaborating with Brands and Partners: Collaborating with brands and partners can open doors to sponsorships, brand deals, and cross-promotion opportunities on YouTube. This section discusses strategies for identifying and approaching potential brand collaborations, establishing mutually beneficial partnerships, negotiating contracts, and maintaining transparency and authenticity in sponsored content. Readers gain insights into leveraging brand collaborations to generate additional income and expand their reach on YouTube.

14.11 Navigating YouTube Policies and Guidelines: Adhering to YouTube's policies and guidelines is essential for maintaining a positive presence on the platform. This section discusses key policies, including copyright, community guidelines, and advertiser-friendly content guidelines. It explores strategies for ensuring compliance, such as respecting intellectual property rights, creating original content, and adhering to ethical practices. Readers gain insights into navigating YouTube's policies and guidelines to protect their channel's reputation and maintain long-term sustainability.

14.12 Scaling and Growing Your YouTube Channel: Scaling and growing a YouTube channel requires continuous effort and adaptation. This section explores strategies for scaling and growing a YouTube channel, including creating series or playlists, diversifying content formats, collaborating with other creators, utilizing YouTube ads, and leveraging emerging trends. It discusses techniques for building a loyal subscriber base, increasing video views and watch time, and expanding the channel's influence and revenue potential.

By the end of Chapter 14, readers have gained a comprehensive understanding of leveraging YouTube for profit. They have learned strategies to create a successful YouTube channel, optimize content for visibility, monetize videos, engage with the audience, analyze performance metrics, navigate policies and guidelines, and scale their YouTube channel for growth. Armed with this knowledge, readers can effectively utilize YouTube as a marketing tool, build a loyal following, and generate revenue through their content and brand partnerships.

CHAPTER 15: MAXIMIZING YOUR EARNINGS WITH PODCASTING

Podcasting has experienced significant growth in recent years, emerging as a popular medium for content consumption and a lucrative opportunity for content creators. Chapter 15 delves into the world of podcasting and explores strategies for maximizing earnings through podcasting endeavors. By understanding the benefits of podcasting, creating high-quality content, growing an engaged audience, monetizing through sponsorships and advertisements, diversifying revenue streams, and leveraging podcasting platforms, readers can unlock the potential of podcasting to generate income and build a thriving podcasting business.

15.1 The Rise of Podcasting: This section highlights the exponential growth and popularity of podcasting as a medium for consuming audio content. It explores the benefits of podcasting, such as its accessibility, portability, and the ability to cater to niche audiences. Readers gain insights into the vast potential of podcasting as an avenue for generating earnings and establishing thought leadership.

15.2 Defining Your Podcasting Niche: Defining a specific podcasting niche is crucial for attracting and engaging a targeted audience. This section guides readers through the process of defining their podcasting niche, including identifying their areas of expertise, researching audience interests, and finding a unique angle or perspective to differentiate their podcast. Readers gain insights into selecting a niche that aligns with their interests and offers value to their target audience.

15.3 Creating High-Quality Podcast Content: High-quality

podcast content is essential for attracting and retaining listeners. This section explores strategies for creating compelling and engaging podcast episodes. It covers aspects such as structuring episodes, conducting thorough research, developing captivating storytelling techniques, incorporating interviews or expert guests, and utilizing appropriate audio editing tools. Readers gain insights into producing content that captivates the audience and establishes their podcast as a valuable resource.

15.4 Growing an Engaged Podcast Audience: Growing an engaged podcast audience is crucial for maximizing earnings. This section discusses strategies for growing a loyal and active listener base. It covers techniques such as promoting the podcast through social media, collaborating with other podcasters or influencers, leveraging email marketing, encouraging listener feedback and reviews, and optimizing podcast discoverability through effective metadata and episode titles. Readers gain insights into fostering audience engagement and attracting new listeners to their podcast.

15.5 Monetizing Through Sponsorships and Advertisements: Monetizing podcasts through sponsorships and advertisements is a common revenue stream for podcasters. This section explores strategies for securing sponsorships and incorporating advertisements into podcast episodes. It covers aspects such as identifying potential sponsors, developing sponsorship packages, negotiating sponsorship agreements, and seamlessly integrating sponsored content into episodes. Readers gain insights into effectively monetizing their podcast through sponsorships and advertisements.

15.6 Diversifying Revenue Streams: Diversifying revenue streams is key to maximizing earnings in podcasting. This section discusses alternative monetization strategies beyond sponsorships and advertisements. It explores techniques such as crowdfunding through platforms like Patreon, offering premium or bonus content for paid subscribers, creating merchandise or branded products, hosting live events or workshops, and exploring affiliate marketing opportunities. Readers gain insights into diversifying their revenue streams and maximizing their earning potential.

15.7 Leveraging Podcasting Platforms: Podcasting platforms play a crucial role in podcast distribution and audience growth. This section explores strategies for leveraging podcasting platforms effectively. It covers aspects such as submitting podcasts to major platforms like Apple Podcasts, Spotify, or Google Podcasts, optimizing podcast descriptions and artwork, utilizing analytics and listener data, and engaging with platform communities. Readers gain insights into leveraging podcasting platforms to expand their reach and attract new listeners.

15.8 Creating a Strong Podcast Brand: Creating a strong podcast brand is essential for building credibility and attracting potential sponsors and advertisers. This section discusses strategies for developing a cohesive and recognizable podcast brand. It explores techniques such as creating a compelling podcast name and logo, maintaining consistent branding across episodes and promotional materials, establishing a unique brand voice, and leveraging social media and other platforms to amplify the podcast's brand presence. Readers gain insights into developing a strong podcast brand that resonates with their target audience and attracts monetization opportunities.

15.9 Collaborating and Networking with Industry Professionals: Collaborating and networking with industry professionals can open doors to valuable opportunities in podcasting. This section explores strategies for building relationships and collaborating with experts, influencers, or fellow podcasters. It covers techniques such as conducting interviews, participating in industry events or conferences, hosting guest episodes, or joining podcasting communities and forums. Readers gain insights into leveraging collaborations and networking to enhance their podcast's credibility and expand their monetization potential.

15.10 Tracking and Analyzing Podcast Performance: Tracking and analyzing podcast performance is crucial for optimizing strategies and identifying areas for improvement. This section discusses key metrics and analytics tools for monitoring podcast performance. It covers aspects such as tracking download numbers, audience demographics, listener engagement, and subscriber growth. Readers gain insights into utilizing data and analytics to refine their podcasting strategies, attract sponsors, and maximize earnings.

15.11 Leveraging Social Media and Digital Marketing: Leveraging social media and digital marketing techniques can significantly boost podcast visibility and audience growth. This section explores strategies for promoting podcasts through social media platforms, creating engaging content, utilizing paid advertising, leveraging email marketing, and optimizing search engine optimization (SEO) techniques. It covers aspects such as creating shareable social media graphics, engaging with listeners on social media, running targeted advertising campaigns, building an email subscriber list, and optimizing podcast website or blog for search engines. Readers gain insights into effectively leveraging digital marketing channels to expand their podcast's reach and attract a larger audience.

15.12 Building a Community and Engaging with Listeners: Building a community around a podcast is vital for establishing a loyal listener base and maximizing earnings. This section discusses strategies for fostering community engagement and actively engaging with listeners. It covers techniques such as creating a podcast website or forum for listeners to connect, hosting live Q&A sessions or virtual events, encouraging listener feedback and reviews, and responding to listener inquiries or comments. Readers gain insights into nurturing a strong podcast community that enhances the overall podcast experience and encourages word-of-mouth promotion.

15.13 Navigating Legal and Copyright Considerations: Navigating legal and copyright considerations is crucial for podcasters to operate within the boundaries of the law and protect their content. This section discusses important legal considerations, such as obtaining appropriate licenses for music or copyrighted material, understanding fair use guidelines, respecting intellectual property rights, and complying with privacy and data protection regulations. Readers gain insights into understanding their rights and responsibilities as podcast creators and ensuring legal compliance in their podcasting endeavors.

15.14 Continuous Learning and Improvement: Continuous learning and improvement are key to sustained success in podcasting. This section explores strategies for staying updated with industry trends, learning from audience feedback, and continually refining podcasting skills. It discusses techniques such as attending industry conferences or webinars, listening to other podcasts for inspiration, seeking mentorship or joining podcasting communities, and investing in professional development resources. Readers gain insights into fostering a growth mindset and continuously improving their podcasting efforts to maximize earnings and stay ahead in the competitive podcasting landscape.

15.15 Scaling and Growing Your Podcasting Business: Scaling and growing a podcasting business requires strategic planning and expansion. This section discusses strategies for scaling podcasting efforts, such as launching additional podcast series or spin-off shows, expanding into new topics or formats, collaborating with influential partners or networks, and exploring sponsorship or advertising opportunities with larger brands. It explores techniques for optimizing workflows, outsourcing tasks, and leveraging automation tools to streamline operations and maximize efficiency. Readers gain insights into scaling their podcasting business and taking it to new heights.

By the end of Chapter 15, readers have gained a comprehensive understanding of maximizing earnings with podcasting. They have learned strategies to create high-quality podcast content, grow an engaged audience, monetize through sponsorships and advertisements, diversify revenue streams, leverage podcasting platforms, build a strong podcast brand, collaborate with industry professionals, track and analyze performance, utilize social media and digital marketing, engage with listeners, navigate legal considerations, embrace continuous learning, and scale their podcasting business. Armed with this knowledge, readers can effectively monetize their podcasts, generate income, and build a sustainable podcasting business.

CHAPTER 16: CONQUERING THE WORLD OF ONLINE ADVERTISING

Online advertising has become an integral part of modern marketing strategies, allowing businesses to reach a global audience and drive targeted traffic to their products or services. Chapter 16 explores the world of online advertising, equipping readers with the knowledge and strategies to conquer this dynamic and ever-evolving landscape. By understanding different advertising platforms, planning effective campaigns, optimizing ad creatives, targeting the right audience, measuring performance, and staying ahead of emerging trends, readers can harness the power of online advertising to achieve their marketing objectives.

16.1 The Evolution of Online Advertising: This section provides an overview of the evolution of online advertising, highlighting its transformation from basic banner ads to highly targeted and interactive campaigns. It discusses the rise of digital advertising platforms, programmatic advertising, and the shift from traditional advertising channels to online mediums. Readers gain insights into the importance of online advertising and its role in reaching and engaging with the digital audience.

16.2 Understanding Online Advertising Platforms: Understanding the various online advertising platforms is crucial for creating effective campaigns. This section explores popular advertising platforms, such as Google Ads, Facebook Ads, Instagram Ads, LinkedIn Ads, Twitter Ads, and YouTube Ads. It delves into the unique features, targeting options, and ad formats offered by each platform, enabling readers to choose the most suitable platforms based on their target audience and advertising goals.

16.3 Planning Effective Online Advertising Campaigns: Planning is essential for successful online advertising campaigns. This section guides readers through the process of planning effective campaigns, including defining campaign objectives, identifying target audience segments, setting realistic budgets, and establishing key performance indicators (KPIs). It discusses the importance of conducting market research, competitor analysis, and keyword research to inform campaign strategy. Readers gain insights into developing a comprehensive plan that aligns with their marketing goals.

16.4 Crafting Compelling Ad Creatives: Compelling ad creatives play a critical role in capturing audience attention and driving engagement. This section explores strategies for crafting effective ad creatives, including attention-grabbing headlines, compelling visuals or videos, persuasive copywriting, and clear calls-to-action (CTAs). It discusses best practices for optimizing ad designs across different platforms and formats. Readers gain insights into creating ad creatives that resonate with their target audience and drive desired actions.

16.5 Targeting the Right Audience: Targeting the right audience is key to maximizing the impact of online advertising campaigns. This section discusses strategies for audience targeting, including demographic targeting, location targeting, interest-based targeting, and behavior-based targeting. It explores advanced targeting options, such as lookalike audiences, remarketing, and custom audience segmentation. Readers gain insights into utilizing targeting features to reach their ideal audience and deliver personalized ad experiences.

16.6 Implementing Conversion Tracking and Analytics: Implementing conversion tracking and analytics is essential for measuring the effectiveness of online advertising campaigns. This section explores techniques for setting up conversion tracking pixels, tags, or codes to monitor key actions, such as website visits, form submissions, or purchases. It discusses the use of analytics platforms, such as Google Analytics, to track campaign performance, monitor website traffic, and analyze user behavior. Readers gain insights into leveraging data and analytics to optimize campaigns and improve return on investment (ROI).

16.7 A/B Testing and Optimization: A/B testing and optimization are critical for maximizing the performance of online advertising campaigns. This section discusses strategies for conducting A/B tests to compare different ad variations, landing pages, or targeting parameters. It explores techniques for analyzing test results, identifying winning elements, and implementing optimizations to improve campaign performance. Readers gain insights into continuously testing and refining their campaigns to achieve better results.

16.8 Budgeting and Bid Management: Effective budgeting and bid management are essential for optimizing campaign spend and achieving desired outcomes. This section explores strategies for setting advertising budgets, allocating funds across campaigns, and managing bids to maximize return on ad spend (ROAS). It discusses bidding options, such as manual bidding, automated bidding, or dynamic bidding, and provides insights into bid optimization techniques. Readers gain insights into efficient budgeting and bid management practices that help them achieve their advertising goals within their allocated resources.

16.9 Exploring Advanced Online Advertising Techniques: This section delves into advanced online advertising techniques that can elevate campaign performance. It discusses strategies such as geotargeting, dayparting, ad scheduling, ad extensions, dynamic retargeting, and personalized messaging. It explores emerging techniques, such as voice search optimization, chatbot advertising, and influencer collaborations. Readers gain insights into staying ahead of the curve and leveraging innovative techniques to gain a competitive edge in online advertising.

16.10 Managing Online Advertising Campaigns: Proper campaign management is crucial for maintaining the effectiveness and efficiency of online advertising efforts. This section discusses strategies for managing campaigns, including monitoring campaign performance, adjusting budgets and bids, optimizing ad targeting, and ensuring compliance with advertising policies. It explores techniques for conducting regular performance reviews, identifying areas for improvement, and implementing necessary adjustments. Readers gain insights into effective campaign management practices that help them achieve their advertising objectives.

16.11 Leveraging Remarketing and Customer Retention: Remarketing and customer retention strategies can significantly impact advertising success. This section explores strategies for leveraging remarketing campaigns to re-engage with previous website visitors or customers. It discusses techniques such as creating tailored ads, offering incentives, and using personalized messaging to nurture customer relationships and drive repeat conversions. Readers gain insights into using remarketing and customer retention strategies to maximize the lifetime value of customers and increase overall advertising ROI.

16.12 Staying Ahead with Online Advertising Trends: Staying ahead of online advertising trends is essential for maintaining a competitive edge. This section explores emerging trends in online advertising, such as influencer marketing, video advertising, native advertising, voice search optimization, artificial intelligence (AI), and machine learning. It discusses the potential of these trends and their impact on future advertising strategies. Readers gain insights into adopting innovative approaches and staying updated with the evolving online advertising landscape.

By the end of Chapter 16, readers have gained a comprehensive understanding of conquering the world of online advertising. They have learned strategies to effectively plan and execute online advertising campaigns, craft compelling ad creatives, target the right audience, track conversions and analyze performance, optimize campaigns, manage budgets and bids, explore advanced techniques, leverage remarketing and customer retention, stay informed about emerging trends, and ultimately maximize their advertising ROI. Armed with this knowledge, readers can navigate the online advertising landscape with confidence and achieve their marketing objectives in the digital realm.

CHAPTER 17: IMPLEMENTING EFFECTIVE EMAIL MARKETING STRATEGIES

Email marketing continues to be a powerful and cost-effective tool for businesses to engage with their audience, nurture customer relationships, and drive conversions. Chapter 17 delves into the world of email marketing, providing readers with a comprehensive understanding of the strategies and best practices for implementing effective email marketing campaigns. By understanding the benefits of email marketing, building targeted email lists, crafting compelling email content, optimizing deliverability, segmenting audiences, automating campaigns, analyzing metrics, and staying compliant with regulations, readers can leverage email marketing to achieve their marketing goals and grow their business.

17.1 The Power of Email Marketing: This section highlights the power of email marketing as a direct and personalized communication channel. It discusses the benefits of email marketing, such as its wide reach, cost-effectiveness, high conversion rates, and ability to nurture customer relationships. Readers gain insights into the potential of email marketing to drive engagement, foster brand loyalty, and generate revenue.

17.2 Building Targeted Email Lists: Building targeted email lists is essential for delivering relevant and personalized content to subscribers. This section explores strategies for building email lists, including opt-in forms on websites, lead magnets, content upgrades, social media promotions, and events. It discusses techniques for segmenting email lists based on subscriber demographics, preferences, or behavior. Readers gain insights into growing their email lists with engaged and interested subscribers.

17.3 Crafting Compelling Email Content: Crafting compelling email content is key to capturing subscribers' attention and driving action. This section discusses strategies for crafting engaging email content, including attention-grabbing subject lines, personalized greetings, persuasive copywriting, and clear calls-to-action (CTAs). It explores different types of email campaigns, such as newsletters, promotional emails, welcome series, abandoned cart emails, and re-engagement campaigns. Readers gain insights into creating email content that resonates with their audience and encourages desired responses.

17.4 Optimizing Email Deliverability: Email deliverability is crucial for ensuring that emails reach subscribers' inboxes and avoid being marked as spam. This section explores strategies for optimizing email deliverability, including maintaining a clean email list, using double opt-ins, implementing email authentication protocols (SPF, DKIM, and DMARC), avoiding spam triggers, and following best practices for email design and coding. Readers gain insights into improving their email deliverability rates and maximizing the chances of their emails being seen by subscribers.

17.5 Segmenting Email Audiences: Segmenting email audiences allows for personalized and targeted messaging, resulting in higher engagement and conversions. This section discusses strategies for segmenting email audiences based on factors such as demographics, purchase history, engagement levels, and preferences. It explores techniques for creating dynamic segments, such as using automation rules and behavioral triggers. Readers gain insights into segmenting their email lists effectively and tailoring their messaging to different audience segments.

17.6 Implementing Email Automation: Email automation streamlines campaign management and allows for timely and relevant communication with subscribers. This section explores strategies for implementing email automation, including welcome series, drip campaigns, cart abandonment sequences, and post-purchase follow-ups. It discusses the benefits of automated email workflows and provides insights into setting up and optimizing automation sequences using email marketing software. Readers gain insights into leveraging automation to deliver targeted and timely messages to their subscribers.

17.7 Designing Mobile-Friendly Emails: Designing mobile-friendly emails is crucial, considering the prevalence of mobile device usage for email consumption. This section discusses strategies for designing emails that render well on various screen sizes, load quickly, and provide a seamless user experience. It covers aspects such as responsive email design, optimizing images, using concise and scannable content, and incorporating mobile-friendly CTAs. Readers gain insights into creating visually appealing and user-friendly emails that cater to mobile users.

17.8 Analyzing Email Metrics: Analyzing email metrics provides valuable insights into the effectiveness of email marketing campaigns. This section explores key email metrics, such as open rates, click-through rates (CTRs), conversion rates, unsubscribe rates, and revenue generated. It discusses techniques for tracking and analyzing these metrics using email marketing software or analytics platforms. Readers gain insights into measuring the success of their email campaigns, identifying areas for improvement, and making data-driven decisions.

17.9 Personalization and Dynamic Content: Personalization and dynamic content enhance the relevance and impact of email marketing campaigns. This section discusses strategies for personalizing email content, such as using merge tags, dynamic content blocks, and personalized recommendations based on subscriber data. It explores techniques for creating personalized subject lines, greetings, and product recommendations. Readers gain insights into leveraging personalization and dynamic content to deliver highly targeted and engaging email experiences.

17.10 Nurturing Customer Relationships: Email marketing is a powerful tool for nurturing customer relationships and fostering loyalty. This section explores strategies for nurturing customer relationships through email, such as sending personalized birthday or anniversary emails, conducting surveys or feedback requests, providing exclusive offers or rewards, and offering educational or informative content. It discusses the importance of maintaining consistent communication and providing value to subscribers. Readers gain insights into building long-term relationships with their email subscribers and turning them into loyal customers.

17.11 Staying Compliant with Regulations: Staying compliant with email marketing regulations is crucial to protect subscriber privacy and maintain ethical practices. This section discusses regulations such as the General Data Protection Regulation (GDPR) and the CAN-SPAM Act. It explores strategies for obtaining explicit consent, providing clear unsubscribe options, including a physical address in emails, and honoring subscribers' preferences. Readers gain insights into adhering to email marketing regulations and building trust with their subscribers.

17.12 Testing and Optimization: Testing and optimization are key to improving the effectiveness of email marketing campaigns. This section discusses strategies for conducting A/B tests to compare different email elements, such as subject lines, CTAs, or email designs. It explores techniques for analyzing test results, identifying winning variations, and implementing optimizations to improve open rates, CTRs, and conversions. Readers gain insights into continuously testing and refining their email campaigns to achieve better results.

17.13 Integration with Other Marketing Channels: Integrating email marketing with other marketing channels can amplify campaign impact and drive results. This section explores strategies for integrating email marketing with social media, content marketing, and other channels. It discusses techniques such as promoting email subscriptions through social media, incorporating email CTAs in blog posts or videos, and leveraging email content to drive social engagement. Readers gain insights into creating cohesive and integrated marketing campaigns that leverage the strengths of different channels.

By the end of Chapter 17, readers have gained a comprehensive understanding of implementing effective email marketing strategies. They have learned strategies to build targeted email lists, craft compelling email content, optimize deliverability, segment audiences, implement automation, analyze metrics, personalize content, nurture customer relationships, comply with regulations, test and optimize campaigns, and integrate email marketing with other channels. Armed with this knowledge, readers can leverage email marketing to engage their audience, drive conversions, and achieve their marketing objectives in a highly competitive digital landscape.

CHAPTER 18: EXPLORING THE WORLD OF CRYPTOCURRENCIES AND BLOCKCHAIN

Cryptocurrencies and blockchain technology have revolutionized the way we perceive and transact with digital assets. Chapter 18 delves into the fascinating world of cryptocurrencies and blockchain, providing readers with a comprehensive understanding of their underlying concepts, the benefits they offer, their potential applications, and the challenges they face. By exploring the fundamentals of cryptocurrencies, understanding blockchain technology, examining different types of cryptocurrencies, discussing their use cases, analyzing market trends, and addressing regulatory considerations, readers can navigate the world of cryptocurrencies and blockchain with confidence.

18.1 Introduction to Cryptocurrencies: This section provides an introduction to cryptocurrencies, explaining their basic concepts and characteristics. It explores the decentralized nature of cryptocurrencies, the role of cryptography in securing transactions, and the use of blockchain technology as the underlying infrastructure. Readers gain insights into the benefits of cryptocurrencies, such as increased transparency, reduced transaction fees, and enhanced security.

18.2 Understanding Blockchain Technology: Blockchain technology forms the backbone of cryptocurrencies, enabling secure and transparent transactions. This section explains the fundamentals of blockchain technology, including distributed ledgers, consensus mechanisms, cryptographic hashing, and smart contracts. It discusses the immutability and transparency provided by blockchain, as well as its potential to revolutionize various industries beyond finance, such as supply chain management, healthcare, and voting systems.

18.3 Exploring Different Types of Cryptocurrencies: The world of cryptocurrencies is vast and diverse, with various types of digital currencies available. This section explores different types of cryptocurrencies, including Bitcoin, Ethereum, Ripple, Litecoin, and others. It discusses their unique features, use cases, and market capitalization. Readers gain insights into the different functionalities and value propositions of each cryptocurrency, as well as their potential for investment or utility purposes.

18.4 Use Cases and Applications of Cryptocurrencies: Cryptocurrencies have found applications beyond traditional financial transactions. This section explores the use cases and applications of cryptocurrencies in areas such as remittances, cross-border payments, decentralized finance (DeFi), non-fungible tokens (NFTs), tokenized assets, and decentralized applications (DApps). It discusses how cryptocurrencies are disrupting traditional industries and empowering individuals with more control over their finances and digital assets.

18.5 Investing and Trading in Cryptocurrencies: Cryptocurrencies have emerged as an investment asset class, attracting investors and traders. This section explores the basics of investing and trading in cryptocurrencies. It discusses strategies for portfolio diversification, conducting fundamental and technical analysis, managing risk, and navigating cryptocurrency exchanges. Readers gain insights into the opportunities and risks associated with investing in cryptocurrencies and the importance of staying informed about market trends and developments.

18.6 Market Trends and Dynamics: The cryptocurrency market is dynamic and influenced by various factors. This section explores market trends and dynamics, such as price volatility, market capitalization, trading volumes, regulatory developments, and technological advancements. It discusses the impact of market trends on cryptocurrency values and investor sentiment. Readers gain insights into understanding the factors that drive the cryptocurrency market and the importance of conducting thorough research and analysis.

18.7 Blockchain Scalability and Interoperability: Scalability and interoperability are significant challenges that blockchain technology faces. This section discusses the scalability limitations of blockchain networks, such as transaction throughput and confirmation times. It explores different solutions and approaches, such as layer 2 solutions, sharding, and off-chain transactions, aimed at improving scalability. It also addresses the importance of interoperability between different blockchain networks to facilitate seamless communication and exchange of digital assets.

18.8 Security and Privacy Considerations: Security and privacy are critical considerations in the cryptocurrency and blockchain space. This section discusses the importance of securing digital wallets, protecting private keys, and understanding the risks associated with hacking, scams, and fraudulent schemes. It explores privacy-enhancing technologies, such as zero-knowledge proofs and secure multi-party computation. Readers gain insights into the measures they can take to ensure the security of their cryptocurrencies and personal information.

18.9 Regulatory Landscape and Considerations: The regulatory landscape surrounding cryptocurrencies and blockchain is evolving and varies across jurisdictions. This section discusses the regulatory considerations, legal frameworks, and compliance requirements related to cryptocurrencies and blockchain-based activities. It explores topics such as anti-money laundering (AML) regulations, know-your-customer (KYC) requirements, taxation, and licensing for cryptocurrency businesses. Readers gain insights into the importance of staying compliant with relevant regulations and understanding the legal implications of engaging in cryptocurrency activities.

18.10 Challenges and Future Perspectives: The world of cryptocurrencies and blockchain faces various challenges on its path to widespread adoption. This section discusses challenges such as regulatory uncertainty, scalability, energy consumption, user experience, and market volatility. It also explores potential future developments, including the integration of cryptocurrencies into mainstream financial systems, advancements in blockchain technology, and the emergence of central bank digital currencies (CBDCs). Readers gain insights into the evolving landscape and the potential impact of cryptocurrencies and blockchain on various industries.

18.11 Ethical and Social Implications: Cryptocurrencies and blockchain technology have ethical and social implications that warrant consideration. This section explores topics such as financial inclusivity, economic empowerment, data privacy, wealth inequality, and the environmental impact of cryptocurrency mining. It discusses the importance of addressing these implications and finding sustainable solutions that promote social good while harnessing the benefits of cryptocurrencies and blockchain.

18.12 Education and Awareness: Education and awareness play a crucial role in the adoption and understanding of cryptocurrencies and blockchain. This section discusses the importance of educating individuals and businesses about the basics of cryptocurrencies, blockchain technology, and the associated risks and opportunities. It explores the role of educational resources, online courses, workshops, and industry events in promoting knowledge and awareness. Readers gain insights into the importance of staying informed and continuously learning about the evolving landscape of cryptocurrencies and blockchain.

18.13 Decentralization and Empowerment: One of the

core principles of cryptocurrencies and blockchain is decentralization, which aims to distribute power and control among network participants. This section explores the concept of decentralization and its potential to empower individuals and communities. It discusses the role of decentralized applications (DApps) and decentralized finance (DeFi) in creating alternative financial systems that promote inclusivity, transparency, and financial sovereignty. Readers gain insights into the transformative power of decentralization and its implications for traditional institutions.

18.14 Sustainability and Energy Consumption: The environmental impact of cryptocurrency mining has raised concerns about sustainability. This section explores the energy consumption associated with cryptocurrency mining and the ongoing efforts to find more sustainable solutions. It discusses the emergence of energy-efficient consensus mechanisms, such as proof-of-stake (PoS), and the exploration of renewable energy sources for mining operations. Readers gain insights into the importance of balancing the benefits of cryptocurrencies with sustainable practices to minimize their environmental footprint.

18.15 Blockchain Beyond Cryptocurrencies: Blockchain technology extends beyond cryptocurrencies and has the potential to revolutionize various industries. This section explores the applications of blockchain in areas such as supply chain management, healthcare, voting systems, intellectual property, and identity management. It discusses the benefits of blockchain in improving transparency, security, and efficiency in these sectors. Readers gain insights into the diverse range of use cases for blockchain technology and its potential to transform traditional processes.

18.16 Emerging Trends and Innovations: The world of cryptocurrencies and blockchain is constantly evolving with emerging trends and innovations. This section explores some of the emerging trends, such as decentralized identity, interoperability between blockchains, blockchain-powered governance, and the integration of blockchain with emerging technologies like artificial intelligence (AI) and the Internet of Things (IoT). It discusses how these trends may shape the future of cryptocurrencies and blockchain and the potential opportunities they present. Readers gain insights into staying updated with emerging trends and preparing for future advancements.

By the end of Chapter 18, readers have gained a comprehensive understanding of exploring the world of cryptocurrencies and blockchain. They have learned about the fundamentals of cryptocurrencies, the underlying technology of blockchain, different types of cryptocurrencies, their use cases and applications, market trends and dynamics, regulatory considerations, ethical and social implications, sustainability concerns, and emerging trends. Armed with this knowledge, readers can navigate the world of cryptocurrencies and blockchain, make informed decisions, and recognize the potential opportunities and challenges that lie ahead.

CHAPTER 19: GENERATING PASSIVE INCOME THROUGH INVESTING

Investing is a powerful tool that allows individuals to grow their wealth and generate passive income over time. Chapter 19 explores the concept of generating passive income through investing, providing readers with a comprehensive understanding of different investment options, strategies, and considerations. By exploring the benefits of passive income, understanding investment vehicles, diversifying portfolios, managing risk, analyzing investment opportunities, and staying informed about market trends, readers can embark on their journey to financial independence and create a sustainable stream of passive income.

19.1 The Power of Passive Income: Passive income refers to income generated with minimal effort or active involvement. This section highlights the benefits of passive income, such as financial independence, flexibility, and the potential to build wealth over time. It discusses the concept of compounding returns and the ability of passive income to provide financial stability and freedom.

19.2 Understanding Different Investment Vehicles: Different investment vehicles offer opportunities for generating passive income. This section explores various investment options, such as stocks, bonds, real estate, mutual funds, exchange-traded funds (ETFs), dividend-paying stocks, peer-to-peer lending, and rental properties. It discusses the characteristics, risks, and potential returns associated with each investment vehicle. Readers gain insights into choosing investment vehicles that align with their financial goals and risk tolerance.

19.3 Diversification and Asset Allocation: Diversification and asset allocation are key principles in building a robust investment portfolio. This section discusses the importance of diversifying investments across different asset classes, industries, and geographical regions to mitigate risks. It explores the concept of asset allocation, balancing investments based on risk tolerance and investment objectives. Readers gain insights into diversifying their portfolios to generate passive income while managing risk effectively.

19.4 Managing Risk and Protecting Capital: Managing risk is essential in investing to safeguard capital and generate sustainable passive income. This section discusses risk management strategies, such as setting realistic return expectations, conducting thorough research, diversifying investments, and using stop-loss orders. It explores the importance of understanding investment risks, including market volatility, inflation, interest rate fluctuations, and geopolitical events. Readers gain insights into managing risk to protect their capital and achieve long-term investment success.

19.5 Analyzing Investment Opportunities: Analyzing investment opportunities is crucial for making informed investment decisions. This section explores techniques for conducting fundamental and technical analysis, including evaluating financial statements, assessing market trends, analyzing industry dynamics, and examining valuation metrics. It discusses the importance of considering risk-reward ratios, growth potential, and income-generating capabilities when evaluating investment opportunities. Readers gain insights into analyzing investment opportunities to identify assets that can generate passive income.

19.6 Building a Dividend Portfolio: Dividend-paying stocks offer a reliable source of passive income. This section explores the concept of dividend investing and discusses strategies for building a dividend portfolio. It covers aspects such as identifying dividend-paying companies, analyzing dividend sustainability, diversifying across sectors, and reinvesting dividends. Readers gain insights into constructing a dividend portfolio that generates regular income and potential capital appreciation.

19.7 Real Estate Investments for Passive Income: Real estate investments offer a tangible and income-generating asset class. This section explores different real estate investment options, such as rental properties, real estate investment trusts (REITs), and real estate crowdfunding. It discusses the benefits of real estate investments, including rental income, potential tax advantages, and potential property value appreciation. Readers gain insights into investing in real estate to generate passive income and build long-term wealth.

19.8 Generating Passive Income through Peer-to-Peer Lending: Peer-to-peer (P2P) lending platforms provide opportunities for individuals to lend money to borrowers and earn interest income. This section explores the concept of P2P lending and discusses strategies for generating passive income through this investment avenue. It covers aspects such as assessing borrower creditworthiness, diversifying loan portfolios, and managing default risks. Readers gain insights into participating in P2P lending as a passive income-generating strategy.

19.9 Leveraging the Power of Index Funds and ETFs: Index funds and exchange-traded funds (ETFs) provide passive investment options that track market indexes. This section explores the benefits of investing in index funds and ETFs, such as diversification, low fees, and ease of management. It discusses strategies for selecting suitable index funds and ETFs based on investment objectives and risk tolerance. Readers gain insights into leveraging index funds and ETFs to generate passive income and participate in broad market growth.

19.10 Staying Informed and Adapting to Market Trends: Staying informed about market trends and adapting investment strategies accordingly is crucial for generating passive income.

This section discusses the importance of continuous learning, keeping up with economic indicators, monitoring industry developments, and adjusting investment portfolios as needed. It explores techniques for staying informed, such as reading financial news, following expert analysis, and utilizing investment research tools. Readers gain insights into staying informed and making informed decisions to optimize their passive income generation.

19.11 Tax Considerations and Optimization: Understanding tax implications and optimizing tax strategies can enhance passive income generation. This section explores tax considerations for different investment vehicles, such as tax-efficient investing, capital gains taxes, dividend taxes, and real estate tax advantages. It discusses techniques for tax optimization, such as using tax-advantaged accounts, timing investment sales, and leveraging tax deductions. Readers gain insights into managing their tax obligations and maximizing their after-tax passive income.

19.12 Managing and Reinvesting Passive Income: Managing and reinvesting passive income are key aspects of building wealth over time. This section explores strategies for managing passive income, including budgeting, tracking expenses, and setting aside reserves for future investments. It discusses the benefits of reinvesting passive income to compound returns and accelerate wealth growth. Readers gain insights into effective management and reinvestment strategies that maximize the long-term potential of their passive income.

19.13 Alternative Investment Opportunities: In addition to traditional investment vehicles, there are alternative investment opportunities that can generate passive income. This section explores alternative investments such as peer-to-peer lending, real estate crowdfunding, royalties, cryptocurrency staking, and angel investing. It discusses the potential risks and rewards associated with these investments and provides insights into diversifying investment portfolios with alternative assets to generate passive income.

19.14 Creating and Managing a Portfolio of Passive Income Streams: Building a portfolio of passive income streams is a strategic approach to generating sustainable income. This section discusses the concept of creating a diversified portfolio of passive income streams by combining different investment vehicles and strategies. It explores techniques for managing and balancing these income streams, assessing their performance, and adjusting investments as needed. Readers gain insights into the process of creating and managing a portfolio that generates reliable passive income.

19.15 Exit Strategies and Capital Preservation: Having exit strategies in place is important to protect capital and ensure financial stability. This section explores different exit strategies for investments, such as selling stocks, exiting real estate investments, or liquidating alternative assets. It discusses the importance of assessing market conditions, monitoring investment performance, and making informed decisions to preserve capital. Readers gain insights into implementing effective exit strategies to safeguard their investments and maintain financial security.

19.16 Continuous Learning and Adaptation: Investing is an ever-evolving landscape, and continuous learning is essential for successful passive income generation. This section emphasizes the importance of staying updated with market trends, industry developments, and regulatory changes. It explores resources for expanding investment knowledge, such as books, courses, seminars, and online communities. Readers gain insights into the mindset of continuous learning and adaptation to navigate the dynamic world of investing.

19.17 Financial Planning and Goal Setting: Financial planning and goal setting provide a roadmap for achieving passive income objectives. This section explores the importance of setting financial goals, creating a budget, and developing a long-term financial plan. It discusses techniques for tracking progress, adjusting goals as circumstances change, and aligning investments with personal aspirations. Readers gain insights into the significance of financial planning and goal setting to achieve passive income milestones.

19.18 Balancing Risk and Return: Investing involves balancing risk and return to optimize passive income generation. This section discusses risk management strategies, including diversification, asset allocation, and understanding risk-reward tradeoffs. It explores techniques for assessing risk tolerance and establishing investment strategies that align with individual risk profiles. Readers gain insights into striking the right balance between risk and return to achieve their passive income goals.

19.19 Embracing Long-Term Investing Mindset: Successful passive income generation often requires a long-term investing mindset. This section emphasizes the importance of patience, discipline, and avoiding emotional decision-making. It explores the benefits of adopting a long-term perspective, such as harnessing the power of compounding returns and riding out market fluctuations. Readers gain insights into cultivating a mindset that aligns with long-term investment goals.

19.20 Monitoring and Adjusting Investment Strategies: Regularly monitoring and adjusting investment strategies is crucial to adapt to changing market conditions. This section discusses techniques for tracking investment performance, analyzing portfolio allocations, and making informed adjustments. It explores the importance of periodic portfolio rebalancing, reassessing risk tolerance, and staying proactive in investment decision-making. Readers gain insights into effectively monitoring and adjusting their investment strategies to optimize passive income generation.

By the end of Chapter 19, readers have gained a comprehensive understanding of generating passive income through investing.

They have explored different investment vehicles, strategies, and considerations, as well as the benefits and challenges associated with passive income generation. Armed with this knowledge, readers can embark on their investment journey, build a diversified portfolio, manage risk effectively, and work towards achieving financial independence through passive income streams.

CHAPTER 20: MASTERING FREELANCING AND REMOTE WORK

The rise of the digital age has brought about significant changes in the way people work and pursue their careers. Chapter 20 explores the world of freelancing and remote work, providing readers with a comprehensive understanding of the opportunities, challenges, and strategies involved in mastering these flexible work arrangements. By delving into the benefits of freelancing and remote work, exploring different freelancing platforms, developing essential skills, managing client relationships, optimizing productivity, and maintaining work-life balance, readers can position themselves for success in the dynamic and evolving landscape of remote work.

20.1 The Rise of Freelancing and Remote Work: This section discusses the increasing popularity of freelancing and remote work arrangements in today's workforce. It explores the factors driving this shift, such as technological advancements, the desire for flexibility, and the changing nature of work. Readers gain insights into the benefits of freelancing and remote work, including independence, work-life balance, location flexibility, and the potential for increased earning potential.

20.2 Understanding Different Freelancing Platforms: Freelancing platforms provide a gateway for connecting freelancers with clients seeking their services. This section explores different freelancing platforms, such as Upwork, Freelancer, Fiverr, and Toptal. It discusses the features, benefits, and target audiences of each platform. Readers gain insights into choosing the right freelancing platforms based on their skills, expertise, and desired work arrangements.

20.3 Developing Essential Freelancing Skills: Successful freelancers possess a set of essential skills that enable them to thrive in their chosen field. This section explores key skills required for freelancing, such as effective communication, time management, self-discipline, adaptability, and problem-solving. It discusses techniques for developing and honing these skills through continuous learning, practice, and seeking feedback. Readers gain insights into cultivating the necessary skills to excel in their freelancing career.

20.4 Building a Strong Freelancer Profile: A strong freelancer profile is crucial for attracting clients and winning projects. This section discusses strategies for creating an impressive freelancer profile, including showcasing relevant skills and experience, highlighting accomplishments, and providing examples of past work. It explores techniques for writing compelling project proposals and effectively communicating value to potential clients. Readers gain insights into crafting a standout freelancer profile that grabs the attention of clients.

20.5 Managing Client Relationships: Effective client relationship management is vital for freelancers to build a strong reputation and secure repeat business. This section explores strategies for managing client relationships, including clear communication, setting expectations, delivering high-quality work, and providing exceptional customer service. It discusses techniques for establishing trust, handling client feedback, and resolving conflicts professionally. Readers gain insights into fostering positive and long-lasting client relationships.

20.6 Pricing and Negotiating Contracts: Determining the right pricing and negotiating contracts are critical aspects of freelancing success. This section discusses strategies for setting fair pricing that aligns with market rates and the value provided. It explores techniques for effectively negotiating contracts, such as understanding client needs, showcasing expertise, and demonstrating the value of the proposed work. Readers gain insights into pricing their services competitively and negotiating contracts that are mutually beneficial.

20.7 Freelancer Financial Management: Effective financial management is essential for freelancers to maintain stability and success in their careers. This section explores strategies for managing freelance finances, including budgeting, tracking income and expenses, saving for taxes, and planning for retirement. It discusses techniques for invoicing clients, managing cash flow, and setting aside emergency funds. Readers gain insights into maintaining financial health as freelancers and optimizing their earnings.

20.8 Productivity and Time Management: Productivity and time management skills are crucial for freelancers to maximize their output and achieve work-life balance. This section explores strategies for enhancing productivity, such as creating effective work routines, setting goals, prioritizing tasks, minimizing distractions, and leveraging productivity tools. It discusses techniques for managing time effectively, including scheduling, batching similar tasks, and delegating when necessary. Readers gain insights into optimizing their productivity and time management as freelancers.

20.9 Building a Professional Network: Building a professional network is valuable for freelancers to expand their opportunities and access a broader pool of clients. This section explores strategies for networking, both online and offline, such as attending industry events, joining professional associations, and engaging in online communities. It discusses the importance of fostering meaningful connections, seeking collaborations, and nurturing relationships with peers and potential clients. Readers gain insights into building a strong professional network that can support their freelancing career.

20.10 Self-Care and Work-Life Balance: Maintaining a healthy work-life balance is crucial for the well-being and sustainability of freelancers. This section explores strategies for self-care, stress management, and creating boundaries between work and personal life. It discusses techniques for setting realistic work hours, taking regular breaks, practicing mindfulness, and engaging in hobbies and activities outside of work. Readers gain insights into prioritizing self-care and achieving a fulfilling work-life balance as freelancers.

20.11 Upskilling and Continuous Learning: Continuous learning and upskilling are essential for freelancers to stay competitive and adapt to changing market demands. This section discusses the importance of staying updated with industry trends, acquiring new skills, and expanding expertise. It explores resources for upskilling, such as online courses, webinars, workshops, and industry certifications. Readers gain insights into the mindset of lifelong learning and investing in their professional development as freelancers.

20.12 Dealing with Challenges and Uncertainty: Freelancing and remote work come with their own set of challenges and uncertainties. This section explores common challenges faced by freelancers, such as finding consistent work, dealing with payment delays, managing multiple clients, and navigating unpredictable income fluctuations. It discusses strategies for overcoming these challenges, including diversifying income streams, building a financial buffer, and maintaining a positive mindset. Readers gain insights into effectively managing the uncertainties that come with freelancing.

By the end of Chapter 20, readers have gained a comprehensive understanding of mastering freelancing and remote work. They have explored the benefits and challenges associated with freelancing, gained insights into different freelancing platforms, developed essential skills, learned strategies for managing client relationships, optimizing productivity, and maintaining work-life balance. Armed with this knowledge, readers can embark on their freelancing journey, build a successful remote career, and leverage the flexibility and opportunities that freelancing and remote work offer.

CHAPTER 21: UNVEILING THE SECRETS OF ONLINE TRADING

Chapter 21 delves into the captivating world of online trading, offering readers a detailed exploration of the secrets, strategies, and intricacies involved in successful trading in the digital era. By understanding the foundations of online trading, exploring different asset classes, mastering technical and fundamental analysis, managing risk, utilizing trading tools, and developing a disciplined trading mindset, readers can unlock the potential for profitable online trading.

21.1 Introduction to Online Trading: This section provides an overview of online trading, explaining its significance in the modern financial landscape. It explores the advantages of online trading, such as accessibility, convenience, and the ability to trade various financial instruments from anywhere in the world. Readers gain insights into the potential opportunities and challenges that come with online trading.

21.2 Building a Strong Trading Foundation: Successful online trading requires a strong foundation of knowledge and understanding. This section explores the key components of building a solid trading foundation, including market terminology, trading platforms, order types, and trading mechanics. It discusses the importance of familiarizing oneself with market dynamics, trading rules, and regulatory considerations. Readers gain insights into the fundamental aspects of online trading that lay the groundwork for success.

21.3 Exploring Different Asset Classes: Online trading encompasses various asset classes, each with its own characteristics and trading strategies. This section explores different asset classes, such as stocks, commodities, foreign exchange (Forex), options, and cryptocurrencies. It discusses the factors that influence price movements in each asset class and the techniques for analyzing their market behavior. Readers gain insights into the diverse opportunities available across different asset classes for profitable trading.

21.4 Technical Analysis and Chart Patterns: Technical analysis is a key tool in online trading, allowing traders to make informed decisions based on historical price patterns and market trends. This section delves into technical analysis techniques, including the identification and interpretation of chart patterns, trend analysis, support and resistance levels, and indicators such as moving averages and oscillators. Readers gain insights into using technical analysis to identify potential trading opportunities and time their trades effectively.

21.5 Fundamental Analysis and Market News: Fundamental analysis focuses on evaluating the intrinsic value of an asset by analyzing economic, financial, and industry factors. This section explores fundamental analysis techniques, including analyzing company financial statements, assessing macroeconomic indicators, and interpreting market news and events. It discusses the impact of fundamental factors on asset prices and how traders can use this information to make informed trading decisions. Readers gain insights into incorporating fundamental analysis into their trading strategies.

21.6 Risk Management Strategies: Managing risk is essential for long-term success in online trading. This section explores risk management strategies, such as setting risk tolerance levels, using stop-loss orders, and employing position sizing techniques. It discusses the importance of diversification, understanding leverage, and maintaining a disciplined approach to risk management. Readers gain insights into mitigating potential losses and protecting capital while maximizing trading opportunities.

21.7 Utilizing Trading Tools and Technology: Online trading platforms offer a wide range of tools and technology to enhance trading efficiency and effectiveness. This section explores trading tools such as real-time market data, charting software, trading algorithms, and automated trading systems. It discusses the benefits and considerations of using these tools and how they can aid in decision-making and trade execution. Readers gain insights into leveraging technology to gain a competitive edge in online trading.

21.8 Developing a Trading Strategy: A well-defined trading strategy is crucial for consistent and profitable trading. This section explores the components of a trading strategy, including defining trading goals, selecting trading timeframes, identifying entry and exit points, and implementing risk management rules. It discusses the importance of backtesting and fine-tuning a trading strategy to align with individual trading styles and preferences. Readers gain insights into developing their personalized trading strategies for online trading success.

21.9 Embracing Emotional Discipline: Emotional discipline is a critical aspect of successful online trading. This section explores the psychological challenges faced by traders, such as fear, greed, and impulsivity. It discusses techniques for developing emotional discipline, including maintaining a trading journal, practicing mindfulness, and implementing pre-defined trading rules. Readers gain insights into managing emotions and maintaining a rational and disciplined mindset while making trading decisions.

21.10 Continuous Learning and Adaptation: Online trading is a dynamic field that requires continuous learning and adaptation. This section emphasizes the importance of staying updated with market trends, technological advancements, and regulatory changes. It explores resources for expanding trading knowledge, such as books, webinars, trading forums, and educational courses. Readers gain insights into the mindset of continuous learning and adapting their trading strategies to evolving market conditions.

21.11 Backtesting and Performance Analysis: Backtesting is a crucial step in evaluating and refining trading strategies. This section explores the process of backtesting, which involves applying a trading strategy to historical market data to assess its performance. It discusses performance analysis techniques, including assessing risk-adjusted returns, win-loss ratios, and drawdowns. Readers gain insights into the importance of objective performance analysis to identify strengths and weaknesses in their trading strategies.

21.12 Trading Psychology and Mindset: A strong trading psychology and mindset are essential for overcoming challenges and maintaining consistency in online trading. This section explores techniques for cultivating a positive and resilient trading mindset, including developing patience, managing expectations, and embracing a growth-oriented mindset. It discusses the role of discipline, confidence, and self-awareness in successful trading. Readers gain insights into harnessing the power of the mind for improved trading performance.

21.13 Trading Ethics and Professionalism: Ethics and professionalism are vital aspects of online trading. This section discusses the importance of ethical trading practices, such as avoiding insider trading, respecting market integrity, and practicing good risk management. It explores the significance of maintaining professionalism in interactions with other traders, brokers, and market participants. Readers gain insights into conducting themselves with integrity and professionalism in their online trading endeavors.

21.14 Developing a Trading Plan and Journal: A trading plan and journal provide structure and accountability in online trading. This section explores the components of a trading plan, including goals, strategies, risk management rules, and trading routines. It discusses the benefits of maintaining a trading journal to track trades, analyze performance, and learn from past experiences. Readers gain insights into developing personalized trading plans and journals to enhance their trading discipline and performance.

21.15 Adapting to Changing Market Conditions: Adapting to changing market conditions is crucial for successful online trading. This section explores techniques for recognizing shifts in market dynamics, adjusting trading strategies, and managing risk in response to changing conditions. It discusses the importance of staying agile, monitoring economic indicators, and being proactive in adapting to evolving market trends. Readers gain insights into the flexibility required to navigate various market conditions.

By the end of Chapter 21, readers have gained a comprehensive understanding of the secrets of online trading. They have explored the foundations of online trading, different asset classes, technical and fundamental analysis techniques, risk management strategies, trading tools and technology, and the importance of mindset and continuous learning. Armed with this knowledge, readers can embark on their online trading journey, apply proven strategies, and unlock the potential for profitable trading in the digital landscape.

CHAPTER 22: MONETIZING YOUR SKILLS THROUGH ONLINE COURSES

Chapter 22 explores the lucrative world of online courses and provides readers with a detailed understanding of how to monetize their skills by creating and selling online courses. By delving into the process of course creation, identifying market demand, designing engaging course content, leveraging online platforms, marketing strategies, and engaging with students, readers can harness the power of e-learning to generate income and share their expertise with a global audience.

22.1 The Rise of Online Learning: This section highlights the growing popularity of online learning and the increasing demand for online courses. It explores the advantages of online learning, such as accessibility, flexibility, and the ability to learn at one's own pace. Readers gain insights into the market potential and opportunities for monetizing their skills through online courses.

22.2 Identifying Your Expertise and Target Audience: Successful online courses start with identifying one's expertise and understanding the target audience. This section discusses techniques for assessing personal strengths, knowledge, and skills to identify areas of expertise. It explores strategies for identifying the target audience, understanding their needs, and tailoring course content to meet their specific requirements. Readers gain insights into aligning their expertise with market demand.

22.3 Defining Course Objectives and Learning Outcomes: Defining clear course objectives and learning outcomes is crucial for designing effective online courses. This section explores techniques for setting course objectives that align with the target audience's needs and expectations. It discusses the importance of establishing measurable learning outcomes that demonstrate the value of the course to potential students. Readers gain insights into defining course objectives and learning outcomes that guide the course creation process.

22.4 Designing Engaging Course Content: Engaging course content is key to attracting and retaining students. This section explores strategies for designing effective course content, including structuring course modules, creating multimedia elements, and incorporating interactive activities. It discusses techniques for presenting information in a clear and concise manner, using storytelling techniques, and incorporating assessments to gauge student progress. Readers gain insights into creating engaging and impactful course content.

22.5 Selecting the Right Online Course Platform: Choosing the right online course platform is essential for effectively delivering and monetizing online courses. This section explores popular online course platforms, such as Udemy, Coursera, Teachable, and Thinkific. It discusses the features, pricing models, and target audiences of each platform. Readers gain insights into selecting the platform that best aligns with their course goals, target audience, and monetization objectives.

22.6 Pricing and Packaging Your Course: Determining the right pricing and packaging strategy is crucial for maximizing course sales. This section discusses techniques for pricing online courses, including considering market demand, assessing the value of the course content, and evaluating competitor pricing. It explores different pricing models, such as one-time payments, subscription-based models, or tiered pricing structures. Readers gain insights into effectively pricing and packaging their courses to attract students and generate revenue.

22.7 Creating Effective Course Marketing Strategies: Effective marketing is key to reaching a wide audience and promoting online courses successfully. This section explores strategies for marketing online courses, including creating compelling course descriptions, utilizing search engine optimization (SEO) techniques, leveraging social media platforms, and utilizing email marketing campaigns. It discusses the importance of building an online presence, engaging with potential students, and utilizing marketing analytics to measure the effectiveness of marketing efforts. Readers gain insights into implementing effective course marketing strategies.

22.8 Engaging with Students and Providing Support: Engaging with students and providing ongoing support is crucial for the success of online courses. This section explores techniques for fostering student engagement, including facilitating discussions, providing timely feedback, and organizing live Q&A sessions. It discusses strategies for managing student expectations, addressing their concerns, and creating a positive learning environment. Readers gain insights into building a supportive and interactive learning community.

22.9 Assessing Course Performance and Iterating: Assessing course performance and making iterative improvements is essential for delivering high-quality online courses. This section explores techniques for collecting student feedback, evaluating course metrics, and analyzing student performance data. It discusses the importance of incorporating student feedback into course updates, addressing areas of improvement, and continuously enhancing the learning experience. Readers gain insights into iterating and improving their courses based on student feedback and performance analysis.

22.10 Protecting Intellectual Property and Copyright: Protecting intellectual property and copyright is crucial when creating and selling online courses. This section explores the importance of understanding copyright laws and obtaining necessary permissions when using third-party content. It discusses strategies for protecting course content from unauthorized distribution, such as utilizing digital rights management

(DRM) tools and watermarking. Readers gain insights into safeguarding their intellectual property and maintaining the integrity of their online courses.

22.11 Leveraging Additional Monetization Strategies: Beyond course sales, there are additional monetization strategies that can enhance the revenue potential of online courses. This section explores strategies such as offering upsells and add-on services, providing coaching or consulting packages, creating membership communities, or developing related products or books. It discusses the benefits and considerations of these monetization strategies. Readers gain insights into diversifying their revenue streams and maximizing the monetization potential of their expertise.

22.12 Continuous Learning and Improvement: Continuous learning and improvement are key to staying ahead in the online course industry. This section emphasizes the importance of staying updated with e-learning trends, emerging technologies, and instructional design principles. It explores resources for expanding knowledge, such as attending webinars, joining online communities, and participating in professional development courses. Readers gain insights into the mindset of continuous learning and adapting their course creation strategies.

By the end of Chapter 22, readers have gained a comprehensive understanding of monetizing their skills through online courses. They have explored the process of course creation, identifying market demand, designing engaging course content, leveraging online platforms, implementing marketing strategies, engaging with students, and continuously improving their courses. Armed with this knowledge, readers can embark on their journey to monetize their skills through online courses, share their expertise with a global audience, and generate income from their passion and knowledge.

CHAPTER 23: BECOMING A SUCCESSFUL VIRTUAL ASSISTANT

Chapter 23 delves into the world of virtual assistance and provides readers with a comprehensive understanding of how to become a successful virtual assistant. By exploring the role of a virtual assistant, acquiring in-demand skills, setting up a virtual assistant business, finding clients, managing client relationships, optimizing productivity, and expanding services, readers can embark on a rewarding career as a virtual assistant.

23.1 The Role of a Virtual Assistant: This section introduces the role of a virtual assistant and its significance in today's digital age. It explores the diverse tasks and responsibilities of a virtual assistant, such as administrative support, customer service, social media management, scheduling, and project coordination. Readers gain insights into the benefits of virtual assistance for businesses and the potential career opportunities available.

23.2 Acquiring In-Demand Skills: Successful virtual assistants possess a range of in-demand skills that make them valuable to clients. This section explores essential skills for virtual assistants, such as communication, organization, time management, technical proficiency, problem-solving, and adaptability. It discusses techniques for acquiring and honing these skills through training, online courses, practice, and seeking feedback. Readers gain insights into developing a skill set that aligns with the needs of virtual assistant clients.

23.3 Setting Up a Virtual Assistant Business: Establishing a virtual assistant business requires careful planning and preparation. This section discusses the steps involved in setting up a virtual assistant business, including defining services, determining pricing, registering a business entity, setting up a home office, and establishing professional systems and processes. It explores strategies for creating a compelling business brand, designing a professional website, and developing a marketing plan. Readers gain insights into building a solid foundation for their virtual assistant business.

23.4 Finding Clients: Finding clients is a crucial aspect of a successful virtual assistant business. This section explores strategies for finding clients, such as leveraging online platforms, networking, referrals, and showcasing expertise through content creation. It discusses techniques for creating an attractive online presence, building a professional network, and utilizing social media platforms to connect with potential clients. Readers gain insights into effective client acquisition strategies for virtual assistants.

23.5 Managing Client Relationships: Maintaining strong client relationships is essential for long-term success as a virtual assistant. This section explores techniques for managing client relationships, including effective communication, understanding client expectations, delivering high-quality work, and providing exceptional customer service. It discusses strategies for setting clear boundaries, managing client feedback, and resolving conflicts professionally. Readers gain insights into building trust, fostering client loyalty, and nurturing long-term partnerships.

23.6 Optimizing Productivity: Optimizing productivity is crucial for managing multiple client tasks and delivering quality work as a virtual assistant. This section explores productivity techniques and tools, such as time blocking, prioritization, task management systems, and automation. It discusses strategies for managing distractions, setting realistic deadlines, and maintaining a healthy work-life balance. Readers gain insights into maximizing productivity and efficiency in their virtual assistant business.

23.7 Expanding Services: Expanding services allows virtual assistants to diversify their income streams and cater to a broader range of client needs. This section explores strategies for expanding services, such as adding new skill sets, offering specialized services, or creating service packages. It discusses techniques for identifying emerging trends and niches in the virtual assistant industry and leveraging them for business growth. Readers gain insights into expanding their service offerings and increasing their value proposition.

23.8 Continuous Learning and Professional Development: Continuous learning and professional development are essential for staying competitive and up-to-date as a virtual assistant. This section emphasizes the importance of staying updated with industry trends, technological advancements, and evolving client needs. It explores resources for expanding knowledge, such as attending webinars, joining professional associations, and participating in relevant training programs. Readers gain insights into the mindset of continuous learning and adapting their skills to meet market demands.

23.9 Managing Finances and Legal Considerations: Managing finances and understanding legal considerations are crucial for running a successful virtual assistant business. This section explores financial management strategies, including budgeting, invoicing, and managing taxes. It discusses legal considerations, such as client contracts, confidentiality agreements, and intellectual property protection. Readers gain insights into maintaining financial stability and ensuring legal compliance in their virtual assistant business.

23.10 Scaling and Outsourcing: Scaling a virtual assistant business involves leveraging resources and outsourcing tasks to accommodate growing client demands. This section explores strategies for scaling a virtual assistant business, such as hiring subcontractors, delegating tasks, or collaborating with other virtual assistants. It discusses techniques for effectively managing a team, maintaining quality control, and optimizing client satisfaction. Readers gain insights into scaling their virtual assistant business for increased profitability and business growth.

23.11 Creating a Positive Professional Image: Creating a positive professional image is essential for attracting clients and building a reputable virtual assistant business. This section explores techniques for maintaining professionalism, such as effective communication, reliability, punctuality, and consistent delivery of high-quality work. It discusses strategies for cultivating a strong online presence, managing online reviews and testimonials, and positioning oneself as an industry expert. Readers gain insights into creating a positive and trustworthy professional image.

23.12 Balancing Personal Well-being: Balancing personal well-being is vital for long-term success and fulfillment as a virtual assistant. This section emphasizes the importance of self-care, setting boundaries, and maintaining a healthy work-life balance. It explores strategies for managing stress, practicing mindfulness, and incorporating self-care routines into daily life. Readers gain insights into prioritizing personal well-being and maintaining a sustainable and rewarding career as a virtual assistant.

By the end of Chapter 23, readers have gained a comprehensive understanding of becoming a successful virtual assistant. They have explored the role of a virtual assistant, acquired in-demand skills, learned how to set up a virtual assistant business, find clients, manage client relationships, optimize productivity, and expand services. Armed with this knowledge, readers can embark on their journey to becoming a successful virtual assistant, delivering value to clients, and building a thriving virtual assistant business.

CHAPTER 24: UNLOCKING THE POWER OF MEMBERSHIP SITES

Chapter 24 delves into the concept of membership sites and provides readers with a comprehensive understanding of how to unlock their power as a business model. By exploring the benefits of membership sites, understanding the components of a successful membership site, creating valuable content, implementing pricing strategies, engaging with members, and optimizing retention, readers can harness the potential of membership sites to generate recurring revenue and build a loyal community of customers.

24.1 Introduction to Membership Sites: This section introduces the concept of membership sites and their significance in the online business landscape. It explores the advantages of membership sites, such as recurring revenue, community building, and customer loyalty. Readers gain insights into the potential opportunities and benefits of leveraging membership sites as a business model.

24.2 Identifying the Right Membership Site Model: Choosing the right membership site model is crucial for success. This section explores different membership site models, such as content-based memberships, community-based memberships, coaching or mentorship programs, and hybrid models. It discusses the characteristics, benefits, and considerations of each model. Readers gain insights into selecting the membership site model that aligns with their business goals and target audience.

24.3 Creating Valuable Content: Delivering valuable content is the backbone of a successful membership site. This section explores strategies for creating content that meets the needs and interests of members. It discusses techniques for developing content pillars, planning content calendars, and utilizing different content formats such as videos, articles, podcasts, or downloadable resources. Readers gain insights into creating content that provides ongoing value and keeps members engaged.

24.4 Designing an Engaging Membership Site: An engaging and user-friendly membership site is essential for member satisfaction. This section explores techniques for designing an intuitive membership site structure, organizing content, and implementing easy navigation. It discusses strategies for creating a visually appealing site that reflects the brand identity and enhances the member experience. Readers gain insights into designing a membership site that captivates and retains members.

24.5 Implementing Pricing Strategies: Choosing the right pricing strategy is crucial for attracting and retaining members. This section explores different pricing models, such as monthly subscriptions, annual memberships, tiered pricing, or one-time fees. It discusses techniques for setting competitive prices that align with the value provided. It also explores strategies for offering free trials, discounts, or incentives to attract new members. Readers gain insights into implementing pricing strategies that optimize revenue and member acquisition.

24.6 Engaging with Members: Building strong relationships with members is essential for the success of a membership site. This section explores strategies for engaging with members, such as interactive discussion forums, live Q&A sessions, member events, or exclusive content releases. It discusses the importance of actively listening to member feedback, addressing their concerns, and providing personalized support. Readers gain insights into fostering a sense of community and creating a positive member experience.

24.7 Driving Member Acquisition: Attracting new members is crucial for the growth of a membership site. This section explores strategies for driving member acquisition, such as content marketing, social media promotion, partnerships, and affiliate programs. It discusses techniques for creating compelling landing pages, utilizing lead magnets, and optimizing search engine visibility. Readers gain insights into implementing effective member acquisition strategies that attract a steady flow of new members.

24.8 Optimizing Member Retention: Retaining members is key to the long-term success of a membership site. This section explores strategies for optimizing member retention, such as delivering ongoing value, providing regular updates and new content, offering member-exclusive perks or discounts, and fostering a sense of belonging within the community. It discusses techniques for implementing retention-focused initiatives, such as automated email sequences, member feedback surveys, or loyalty programs. Readers gain insights into maintaining member loyalty and reducing churn.

24.9 Leveraging Upsells and Cross-Sells: Upselling and cross-selling strategies can enhance the revenue potential of a membership site. This section explores techniques for leveraging upsells and cross-sells, such as offering premium upgrades, additional products or services, or exclusive access to advanced features. It discusses the importance of understanding member needs and preferences to tailor upsell and cross-sell offers effectively. Readers gain insights into maximizing the revenue potential of their membership site through strategic upselling and cross-selling.

24.10 Analyzing Metrics and Making Data-Driven Decisions: Analyzing key metrics is essential for monitoring the health and performance of a membership site. This section explores important metrics to track, such as member retention rates, churn rates, engagement levels, and revenue growth. It discusses the tools and techniques for collecting and analyzing data to make informed decisions and drive improvements. Readers gain insights into using data to optimize their membership site's performance.

24.11 Continuously Improving the Membership Site: Continuous improvement is crucial for staying competitive and meeting member expectations. This section emphasizes the importance of actively seeking member feedback, monitoring industry trends, and incorporating member suggestions into ongoing site enhancements. It explores techniques for conducting member surveys, A/B testing, and implementing iterative improvements. Readers gain insights into cultivating a culture of continuous improvement and staying ahead in the membership site landscape.

24.12 Scaling and Automating Operations: Scaling a membership site involves optimizing operations to accommodate growth. This section explores strategies for scaling and automating membership site operations, such as utilizing membership site platforms with built-in automation features, outsourcing non-core tasks, or implementing efficient content production processes. It discusses techniques for managing increased member volumes, maintaining service quality, and optimizing resource utilization. Readers gain insights into scaling their membership site for sustainable growth.

By the end of Chapter 24, readers have gained a comprehensive understanding of unlocking the power of membership sites. They have explored the benefits of membership sites, understood the components of a successful membership site, learned strategies for creating valuable content, implementing pricing strategies, engaging with members, optimizing retention, and scaling operations. Armed with this knowledge, readers can embark on their journey to harness the potential of membership sites, build a thriving community of members, and generate recurring revenue from their expertise and offerings.

CHAPTER 25: EXPLORING THE POTENTIAL OF ONLINE COACHING AND CONSULTING

Chapter 25 delves into the world of online coaching and consulting, providing readers with a comprehensive understanding of the potential and opportunities in this growing industry. By exploring the benefits of online coaching and consulting, defining target clients, developing expertise, structuring services, marketing strategies, delivering impactful sessions, and building long-term client relationships, readers can harness the power of virtual coaching and consulting to create a fulfilling and profitable career.

25.1 Introduction to Online Coaching and Consulting: This section introduces the concept of online coaching and consulting and its significance in the digital age. It explores the advantages of virtual coaching and consulting, such as flexibility, global reach, and scalability. Readers gain insights into the potential opportunities and benefits of leveraging online platforms to offer their expertise and guidance.

25.2 Defining Target Clients: Defining target clients is crucial for the success of online coaching and consulting. This section explores techniques for identifying the ideal client profile, considering factors such as demographics, needs, and challenges. It discusses the importance of understanding target clients' pain points and aspirations to tailor services effectively. Readers gain insights into defining their niche and targeting clients who will benefit most from their expertise.

25.3 Developing Expertise and Specialization: Building expertise and specialization is essential for establishing credibility as an online coach or consultant. This section explores strategies for developing expertise, such as continuous learning, staying updated with industry trends, attending relevant training programs, and acquiring certifications. It discusses the benefits of specializing in a particular area and positioning oneself as an expert in that domain. Readers gain insights into honing their skills and knowledge to offer high-quality services.

25.4 Structuring Coaching and Consulting Services: Structuring coaching and consulting services is critical for providing clarity and value to clients. This section explores different service models, such as one-on-one coaching, group coaching, workshops, or consulting packages. It discusses techniques for defining service offerings, setting pricing, and establishing clear deliverables and expectations. Readers gain insights into structuring services that align with their expertise and target clients' needs.

25.5 Building a Strong Online Presence: Creating a strong online presence is essential for attracting clients and establishing credibility in the online coaching and consulting industry. This section explores strategies for building an effective personal brand, including creating a professional website, optimizing social media profiles, and showcasing testimonials and case studies. It discusses techniques for content creation, such as blog posts, videos, or podcasts, to demonstrate expertise and attract potential clients. Readers gain insights into building a compelling online presence that resonates with their target audience.

25.6 Implementing Marketing Strategies: Implementing effective marketing strategies is crucial for promoting online coaching and consulting services. This section explores techniques for marketing, such as content marketing, search engine optimization (SEO), email marketing, partnerships, and social media advertising. It discusses strategies for identifying target clients, crafting compelling messages, and leveraging various marketing channels to reach the intended audience. Readers gain insights into implementing a tailored marketing plan to generate leads and convert them into clients.

25.7 Delivering Impactful Coaching and Consulting Sessions: Delivering impactful sessions is the cornerstone of a successful online coaching and consulting practice. This section explores techniques for conducting effective coaching and consulting sessions, such as active listening, asking powerful questions, providing guidance, and offering actionable strategies. It discusses the importance of creating a safe and supportive environment for clients to explore their goals and challenges. Readers gain insights into delivering transformative sessions that help clients achieve their desired outcomes.

25.8 Building Client Relationships: Building strong client relationships is essential for client satisfaction and long-term success in online coaching and consulting. This section explores strategies for fostering meaningful connections with clients, such as regular check-ins, personalized support, and providing ongoing value beyond sessions. It discusses techniques for managing client expectations, addressing concerns, and maintaining open lines of communication. Readers gain insights into building trust and loyalty with clients to establish a sustainable coaching and consulting business.

25.9 Implementing Feedback and Evaluation: Implementing feedback and evaluation processes is crucial for continuous improvement in online coaching and consulting. This section explores techniques for soliciting client feedback, such as feedback surveys or post-session evaluations. It discusses the importance of actively seeking feedback to identify areas for improvement and enhance the client experience. Readers gain insights into leveraging client feedback to refine their coaching and consulting approaches.

25.10 Scaling and Expanding Services: Scaling and expanding services enable coaches and consultants to reach a broader audience and increase revenue potential. This section explores strategies for scaling an online coaching and consulting practice, such as creating digital products, offering group programs, or hiring additional team members. It discusses techniques for optimizing time and resource utilization while maintaining service quality. Readers gain insights into scaling their business while continuing to deliver impactful services.

25.11 Managing Finances and Legal Considerations: Managing finances and understanding legal considerations are vital for running a successful online coaching and consulting business. This section explores strategies for financial management, such as budgeting, invoicing, and managing taxes. It discusses legal considerations, such as client contracts, liability protection, and intellectual property rights. Readers gain insights into maintaining financial stability and legal compliance in their coaching and consulting practice.

25.12 Cultivating Professional Development: Continuous professional development is essential for staying ahead in the online coaching and consulting industry. This section emphasizes the importance of staying updated with industry trends, acquiring new skills, and seeking professional development opportunities. It explores resources for expanding knowledge, such as attending conferences, joining professional associations, and participating in coaching or consulting training programs. Readers gain insights into cultivating a growth mindset and continuously improving their skills and expertise.

By the end of Chapter 25, readers have gained a comprehensive understanding of the potential of online coaching and consulting. They have explored the benefits of virtual coaching and consulting, defined target clients, developed expertise, structured services, implemented marketing strategies, delivered impactful sessions, and built long-term client relationships. Armed with this knowledge, readers can embark on their journey to harness the power of online coaching and consulting, make a positive impact on clients' lives, and build a thriving and fulfilling career.

CHAPTER 26: CREATING AND SELLING SOFTWARE AS A SERVICE (SAAS)

Chapter 26 explores the world of Software as a Service (SaaS) and provides readers with a comprehensive understanding of how to create and sell SaaS products. By delving into the SaaS business model, identifying market opportunities, developing a SaaS product, pricing strategies, marketing tactics, customer acquisition, and retention strategies, readers can harness the potential of SaaS to build a successful and scalable software business.

26.1 Introduction to Software as a Service (SaaS): This section introduces the concept of Software as a Service (SaaS) and its significance in the software industry. It explores the advantages of the SaaS business model, such as accessibility, scalability, and cost-effectiveness. Readers gain insights into the potential opportunities and benefits of leveraging SaaS to create and sell software products.

26.2 Identifying Market Opportunities: Identifying market opportunities is crucial for the success of a SaaS product. This section explores techniques for market research, understanding customer pain points, and identifying gaps in existing software solutions. It discusses strategies for conducting competitive analysis, surveying potential customers, and utilizing market research tools. Readers gain insights into identifying market needs and opportunities for their SaaS product.

26.3 Developing a SaaS Product: Developing a SaaS product requires careful planning and execution. This section explores the process of developing a SaaS product, including defining the product concept, designing the user interface (UI) and user experience (UX), selecting the technology stack, and building a scalable infrastructure. It discusses strategies for agile development, incorporating user feedback, and ensuring security and data privacy. Readers gain insights into the product development process for a SaaS offering.

26.4 Pricing Strategies for SaaS: Choosing the right pricing strategy is essential for the success and profitability of a SaaS product. This section explores different pricing models commonly used in SaaS, such as subscription-based pricing, tiered pricing, usage-based pricing, or freemium models. It discusses techniques for pricing optimization, including considering market demand, competitor analysis, and customer value metrics. Readers gain insights into setting competitive and sustainable pricing for their SaaS product.

26.5 Marketing and Positioning a SaaS Product: Effective marketing and positioning strategies are crucial for attracting customers to a SaaS product. This section explores techniques for marketing and positioning a SaaS product, such as creating a compelling value proposition, identifying target customer segments, and developing marketing messages that highlight the unique features and benefits of the product. It discusses strategies for content marketing, search engine optimization (SEO), social media marketing, and paid advertising. Readers gain insights into positioning their SaaS product effectively in the market.

26.6 Customer Acquisition for SaaS: Acquiring customers is a key aspect of selling a SaaS product. This section explores customer acquisition strategies for SaaS, including inbound marketing, lead generation, partnerships, and referral programs. It discusses techniques for creating a sales funnel, optimizing conversion rates, and leveraging marketing automation tools. It also explores the importance of customer onboarding and providing a seamless user experience. Readers gain insights into acquiring customers and driving user adoption for their SaaS product.

26.7 Retention and Customer Success Strategies: Retaining customers and ensuring their success is vital for the long-term profitability of a SaaS product. This section explores retention and customer success strategies, such as providing excellent customer support, offering regular product updates and enhancements, and implementing customer feedback loops. It discusses techniques for measuring customer satisfaction, reducing churn rates, and fostering customer loyalty. Readers gain insights into optimizing customer retention and maximizing the lifetime value of their SaaS customers.

26.8 Scaling Infrastructure and Operations: Scaling the infrastructure and operations is necessary to support the growth of a SaaS product. This section explores strategies for scaling the infrastructure, such as leveraging cloud computing platforms, implementing scalable databases, and ensuring high availability and performance. It discusses techniques for optimizing resource utilization, monitoring system health, and automating repetitive tasks. Readers gain insights into scaling their SaaS product to accommodate increasing user demand.

26.9 Ensuring Security and Data Privacy: Ensuring the security and data privacy of a SaaS product is of paramount importance. This section explores strategies for implementing robust security measures, such as data encryption, user authentication, and access control. It discusses techniques for complying with data protection regulations, such as the General Data Protection Regulation (GDPR) or the California Consumer Privacy Act (CCPA). Readers gain insights into safeguarding customer data and maintaining trust in their SaaS product.

26.10 Analytics and Data-Driven Decision Making: Leveraging analytics and data-driven decision-making is crucial for optimizing the performance of a SaaS product. This section explores techniques for collecting and analyzing user data, such as product usage metrics, customer behavior, and conversion rates. It discusses the importance of tracking key performance indicators (KPIs) and using data to inform product enhancements, marketing strategies, and customer success initiatives. Readers gain insights into leveraging analytics to drive continuous improvement in their SaaS product.

26.11 Managing Customer Feedback and Iterating: Managing customer feedback and iterating on the product is essential for meeting customer needs and staying competitive in the SaaS industry. This section explores techniques for gathering customer feedback, such as surveys, user testing, and customer support interactions. It discusses strategies for prioritizing and implementing customer-driven product enhancements and iterative improvements. Readers gain insights into fostering a customer-centric approach to product development and refining their SaaS offering based on customer feedback.

26.12 Cultivating a Supportive SaaS Community: Building a supportive SaaS community enhances customer engagement and loyalty. This section explores strategies for creating a community around the SaaS product, such as user forums, knowledge bases, and customer events. It discusses the importance of facilitating interactions among customers, encouraging knowledge sharing, and providing avenues for user feedback and collaboration. Readers gain insights into cultivating a vibrant and supportive community around their SaaS product.

By the end of Chapter 26, readers have gained a comprehensive understanding of creating and selling Software as a Service (SaaS). They have explored the SaaS business model, identified market opportunities, developed a SaaS product, implemented pricing and marketing strategies, acquired and retained customers, scaled infrastructure, ensured security and data privacy, leveraged analytics, managed customer feedback, and cultivated a supportive community. Armed with this knowledge, readers can embark on their journey to create and sell their own SaaS product, offering value to customers and building a successful software business.

CHAPTER 27: MAKING MONEY WITH ONLINE SURVEYS AND MARKET RESEARCH

Chapter 27 delves into the world of online surveys and market research, providing readers with a comprehensive understanding of how to make money by participating in online surveys and engaging in market research activities. By exploring the benefits of online surveys, understanding market research methodologies, finding legitimate survey platforms, maximizing earnings, and optimizing participation, readers can leverage their opinions and insights to generate income through online surveys and market research opportunities.

27.1 Introduction to Online Surveys and Market Research: This section introduces the concept of online surveys and market research and their significance in the business world. It explores the role of consumer opinions and insights in shaping products, services, and marketing strategies. Readers gain insights into the potential opportunities and benefits of participating in online surveys and market research activities.

27.2 The Benefits of Online Surveys: Online surveys offer several benefits to participants. This section explores the advantages of online surveys, such as flexibility, convenience, and the ability to share opinions from the comfort of one's own home. It discusses how online surveys provide individuals with a platform to influence the development of products and services and shape consumer trends. Readers gain insights into the benefits of participating in online surveys and the potential impact of their opinions.

27.3 Understanding Market Research Methodologies: Market research encompasses various methodologies and approaches.

This section explores different market research methodologies, such as surveys, focus groups, interviews, and observational studies. It discusses how these methodologies provide businesses with valuable insights into consumer preferences, behaviors, and attitudes. Readers gain insights into the different research techniques employed by businesses and the role of online surveys within the broader field of market research.

27.4 Finding Legitimate Survey Platforms: Finding legitimate survey platforms is crucial for earning money through online surveys. This section explores strategies for identifying reputable survey platforms, including conducting research, reading reviews, and considering factors such as payment methods, survey frequency, and user feedback. It discusses the importance of registering with reliable platforms that respect participant privacy and provide fair compensation for survey completion. Readers gain insights into finding trustworthy survey platforms to maximize their earning potential.

27.5 Maximizing Earnings from Online Surveys: Maximizing earnings from online surveys requires a strategic approach. This section explores techniques for increasing survey opportunities, such as signing up for multiple survey platforms, completing profile questionnaires, and regularly checking for new survey invitations. It discusses strategies for qualifying for higher-paying surveys by providing accurate and detailed responses. Readers gain insights into maximizing their earning potential by optimizing their participation in online surveys.

27.6 Participating in Focus Groups and Product Testing: Beyond online surveys, participating in focus groups and product testing can offer additional income opportunities. This section explores the benefits of participating in focus groups and product testing, including the ability to provide direct feedback on new products and services. It discusses strategies for finding focus group opportunities and product testing programs. Readers gain insights into diversifying their market research participation and expanding their income potential.

27.7 Engaging in Mystery Shopping: Mystery shopping provides a unique way to earn money and contribute to market research efforts. This section explores the concept of mystery shopping, where individuals are hired to evaluate and provide feedback on the customer experience in various establishments. It discusses strategies for finding legitimate mystery shopping opportunities and provides tips for conducting effective evaluations. Readers gain insights into the world of mystery shopping as a source of income and market research feedback.

27.8 Managing Time and Expectations: Managing time and expectations is crucial when engaging in online surveys and market research activities. This section explores strategies for balancing survey participation with other commitments and setting realistic expectations for earnings. It discusses the importance of being consistent, maintaining a schedule, and avoiding scams or low-paying opportunities. Readers gain insights into effectively managing their time and expectations to optimize their earning potential.

27.9 Providing Honest and Thoughtful Feedback: Providing honest and thoughtful feedback is essential for the success of online surveys and market research. This section explores the importance of providing accurate and detailed responses in surveys, focus groups, and product testing activities. It discusses strategies for offering constructive feedback and valuable insights that can help businesses improve their products and services. Readers gain insights into the role of their opinions and feedback in driving meaningful market research outcomes.

27.10 Protecting Privacy and Avoiding Scams: Protecting privacy and avoiding scams is paramount when participating in online surveys and market research. This section explores strategies for safeguarding personal information, including using reputable survey platforms, being cautious of suspicious requests, and understanding privacy policies. It discusses tips for recognizing and avoiding survey scams that may compromise personal data or exploit participants. Readers gain insights into protecting their privacy and ensuring a safe and legitimate online survey experience.

27.11 Exploring Additional Market Research Opportunities: Beyond online surveys, there are various additional market research opportunities that individuals can explore. This section highlights alternative market research activities, such as participating in online communities, joining feedback panels, or becoming a brand ambassador. It discusses the benefits and potential earnings associated with these opportunities. Readers gain insights into diversifying their market research participation and exploring new avenues for income generation.

27.12 Leveraging Market Research Skills: Engaging in market research activities can develop valuable skills that extend beyond earning money. This section explores the skills acquired through online surveys and market research, such as critical thinking, data analysis, and communication. It discusses how these skills can be leveraged in other areas, such as freelance market research consulting or pursuing careers in consumer insights. Readers gain insights into the long-term value of participating in market research activities.

By the end of Chapter 27, readers have gained a comprehensive understanding of making money with online surveys and market research. They have explored the benefits of online surveys, understood market research methodologies, learned strategies for finding legitimate survey platforms, maximizing earnings, managing time and expectations, protecting privacy, and exploring additional market research opportunities. Armed with this knowledge, readers can embark on their journey to leverage their opinions and insights, earn money through online surveys, and actively contribute to market research efforts.

CHAPTER 28: CAPITALIZING ON DOMAIN FLIPPING AND WEBSITE FLIPPING

Chapter 28 explores the lucrative opportunities of domain flipping and website flipping, providing readers with a comprehensive understanding of how to capitalize on these practices to generate profits. By delving into the world of domain flipping and website flipping, understanding the market dynamics, acquiring valuable domains and websites, optimizing their value, and executing successful flips, readers can leverage their knowledge and skills to build a profitable business in the digital marketplace.

28.1 Introduction to Domain Flipping and Website Flipping: This section introduces the concepts of domain flipping and website flipping and highlights their significance in the digital landscape. It explores the opportunities presented by buying and selling valuable domain names and websites. Readers gain insights into the potential benefits and profitability of capitalizing on domain flipping and website flipping.

28.2 Understanding the Market Dynamics: Understanding the market dynamics is crucial for successful domain flipping and website flipping. This section explores the factors that influence the value of domains and websites, such as domain name relevance, keyword popularity, website traffic, revenue generation, and market demand. It discusses the importance of conducting market research, monitoring trends, and staying updated with industry developments. Readers gain insights into the market forces that drive the buying and selling of domains and websites.

28.3 Acquiring Valuable Domains: Acquiring valuable domains

is the foundation of domain flipping. This section explores strategies for identifying and acquiring high-quality domain names, such as keyword research, domain auctions, expired domain marketplaces, and private acquisitions. It discusses techniques for evaluating the potential value of domains based on factors like domain age, keyword relevance, brandability, and market demand. Readers gain insights into acquiring valuable domains that have the potential for profitable flips.

28.4 Enhancing Domain Value: Enhancing the value of acquired domains is essential for maximizing profits in domain flipping. This section explores techniques for increasing the value of domains, such as improving search engine optimization (SEO), creating landing pages, building backlinks, and developing a brand identity. It discusses the importance of domain monetization strategies, such as affiliate marketing, pay-per-click (PPC) advertising, or leasing domains to generate revenue while waiting for a sale. Readers gain insights into optimizing the value of their acquired domains.

28.5 Selling Domains: Selling domains at the right time and through the right channels is critical for successful domain flipping. This section explores strategies for selling domains, such as utilizing domain marketplaces, engaging with domain brokers, reaching out to potential buyers directly, or listing domains on auction platforms. It discusses techniques for setting competitive prices, negotiating deals, and creating effective sales listings. Readers gain insights into the process of selling domains to maximize their profitability.

28.6 Acquiring Valuable Websites: Acquiring valuable websites is the foundation of website flipping. This section explores strategies for identifying and acquiring websites with growth potential, such as market research, due diligence, and assessing factors like website traffic, revenue streams, content quality, and monetization methods. It discusses techniques for evaluating the website's potential for improvement and future profitability. Readers gain insights into acquiring websites that have the potential for successful flips.

28.7 Enhancing Website Value: Enhancing the value of acquired websites is crucial for maximizing profits in website flipping. This section explores techniques for improving website performance, such as optimizing SEO, enhancing user experience (UX), refining content quality, and expanding monetization strategies. It discusses the importance of analyzing website analytics, identifying growth opportunities, and implementing effective marketing strategies. Readers gain insights into enhancing the value of their acquired websites.

28.8 Selling Websites: Selling websites at the right time and through the right channels is vital for successful website flipping. This section explores strategies for selling websites, such as utilizing website marketplaces, engaging with website brokers, reaching out to potential buyers directly, or listing websites on auction platforms. It discusses techniques for setting competitive prices, preparing comprehensive sales documentation, and effectively marketing the website to attract potential buyers. Readers gain insights into the process of selling websites to maximize their profitability.

28.9 Assessing Risks and Mitigating Challenges: Assessing risks and mitigating challenges is essential when engaging in domain flipping and website flipping. This section explores the potential risks and challenges associated with these practices, such as market volatility, legal issues, fraudulent transactions, or unforeseen technical issues with websites. It discusses techniques for conducting thorough due diligence, securing transactions, and implementing risk management strategies. Readers gain insights into safeguarding their investments and minimizing potential challenges.

28.10 Scaling Domain and Website Flipping Operations: Scaling domain and website flipping operations enables entrepreneurs to increase their profitability and expand their business. This section explores strategies for scaling operations, such as streamlining acquisition processes, leveraging automation tools, and outsourcing certain tasks. It discusses techniques for managing a portfolio of domains and websites, optimizing workflow efficiency, and diversifying investments. Readers gain insights into scaling their domain and website flipping endeavors.

28.11 Staying Updated and Adapting to Trends: Staying updated with industry trends and adapting to market changes is vital for long-term success in domain flipping and website flipping. This section emphasizes the importance of continuous learning, networking with industry professionals, and monitoring market dynamics. It discusses techniques for identifying emerging trends, exploring new niches, and adjusting strategies accordingly. Readers gain insights into cultivating a growth mindset and staying ahead in the dynamic domain and website flipping landscape.

28.12 Nurturing Relationships and Building a Reputation: Nurturing relationships and building a strong reputation in the domain and website flipping community can lead to new opportunities and increased trust from buyers and sellers. This section explores strategies for networking, engaging in online communities, and providing exceptional customer service. It discusses techniques for maintaining positive relationships with buyers, sellers, and industry professionals. Readers gain insights into fostering a positive reputation and building a network of contacts in the domain and website flipping industry.

By the end of Chapter 28, readers have gained a comprehensive understanding of capitalizing on domain flipping and website flipping. They have explored the market dynamics, learned strategies for acquiring valuable domains and websites, optimizing their value, executing successful flips, and mitigating risks. Armed with this knowledge, readers can embark on their journey to capitalize on domain flipping and website flipping, leveraging their skills and insights to build a profitable business in the digital marketplace.

CHAPTER 29: MASTERING THE ART OF ONLINE AUCTIONS AND MARKETPLACES

Chapter 29 delves into the world of online auctions and marketplaces, providing readers with a comprehensive understanding of how to master the art of buying and selling on these platforms. By exploring the dynamics of online auctions and marketplaces, understanding the strategies for successful bidding and selling, leveraging effective listing techniques, optimizing pricing and product descriptions, and managing customer interactions, readers can become adept at navigating the digital marketplace and maximizing their profits.

29.1 Introduction to Online Auctions and Marketplaces: This section introduces the concept of online auctions and marketplaces and highlights their significance in the e-commerce landscape. It explores the benefits and opportunities presented by online platforms for buying and selling various products. Readers gain insights into the potential of online auctions and marketplaces for generating income and reaching a wide customer base.

29.2 Understanding the Dynamics of Online Auctions: Understanding the dynamics of online auctions is essential for successful bidding and buying. This section explores the intricacies of online auctions, including the different auction formats, bidding strategies, and the concept of bidding increments. It discusses the importance of conducting market research, setting bidding limits, and timing bids strategically. Readers gain insights into the strategies and tactics that can lead to successful bidding and winning auctions.

29.3 Strategies for Successful Bidding: Developing effective bidding strategies is crucial for securing desired items at favorable prices in online auctions. This section explores techniques for strategic bidding, such as sniping (placing bids at the last moment), incremental bidding, and setting maximum bid limits. It discusses the importance of monitoring auctions, assessing competitors, and recognizing bid patterns. Readers gain insights into developing personalized bidding strategies that increase their chances of winning auctions.

29.4 Selling on Online Auctions and Marketplaces: Selling products on online auctions and marketplaces requires strategic planning and execution. This section explores strategies for successful selling, such as identifying popular products, researching market demand, and selecting the appropriate auction format or listing type. It discusses techniques for optimizing product listings, including compelling titles, detailed descriptions, high-quality images, and competitive pricing. Readers gain insights into maximizing their selling potential on online platforms.

29.5 Leveraging Effective Listing Techniques: Creating compelling product listings is crucial for attracting potential buyers and driving sales. This section explores effective listing techniques, such as crafting attention-grabbing titles, providing accurate and detailed descriptions, using high-quality images, and highlighting unique selling points. It discusses strategies for optimizing listings for search engines and leveraging keywords to increase visibility. Readers gain insights into creating persuasive and informative product listings.

29.6 Optimizing Pricing and Product Descriptions: Pricing products appropriately and creating compelling product descriptions are key factors in attracting buyers and maximizing profits. This section explores strategies for pricing products competitively, considering factors such as market demand, product condition, and competitor prices. It discusses techniques for writing persuasive and informative product descriptions that highlight features, benefits, and usage instructions. Readers gain insights into optimizing pricing and product descriptions to drive conversions.

29.7 Managing Customer Interactions: Providing excellent customer service and managing customer interactions are vital for building a positive reputation and generating repeat business. This section explores strategies for effective communication with customers, including timely responses to inquiries, providing accurate information, and addressing concerns or issues promptly. It discusses techniques for resolving disputes, managing returns or refunds, and cultivating positive feedback. Readers gain insights into fostering positive customer interactions and maintaining high customer satisfaction levels.

29.8 Expanding Reach through Multiple Platforms: Expanding reach by utilizing multiple online auction and marketplace platforms can increase exposure and potential sales. This section explores strategies for diversifying selling efforts across various platforms, such as eBay, Amazon, Etsy, or specialized niche marketplaces. It discusses the benefits of cross-listing products, managing inventory effectively, and leveraging platform-specific marketing tools. Readers gain insights into expanding their reach and accessing a broader customer base through multiple platforms.

29.9 Leveraging Auction and Marketplace Tools: Auction and marketplace tools can enhance efficiency and optimize selling efforts. This section explores various tools and software available to sellers, such as listing management tools, inventory tracking systems, and automated pricing tools. It discusses the benefits of using analytics and reporting features to monitor performance, track sales trends, and identify opportunities for improvement. Readers gain insights into leveraging technology to streamline their auction and marketplace operations.

29.10 Adapting to Market Trends and Dynamics: Adapting to market trends and dynamics is crucial for staying competitive in online auctions and marketplaces. This section emphasizes the importance of staying updated with market trends, monitoring competitor activities, and adjusting strategies accordingly. It discusses techniques for identifying emerging product trends, exploring new categories, and capitalizing on seasonal or timely opportunities. Readers gain insights into cultivating adaptability and agility to thrive in the ever-changing online marketplace.

29.11 Building a Reputation and Brand: Building a positive reputation and brand presence is vital for long-term success in online auctions and marketplaces. This section explores strategies for cultivating a strong reputation, including consistently delivering high-quality products, providing exceptional customer service, and actively seeking positive feedback. It discusses techniques for building brand awareness, such as creating a distinctive brand identity and utilizing branding elements in product listings. Readers gain insights into nurturing a positive reputation and establishing a trusted brand.

29.12 Continuous Learning and Improvement: Continuous learning and improvement are essential for mastering the art of online auctions and marketplaces. This section emphasizes the importance of staying updated with platform policies, industry developments, and evolving customer preferences. It discusses the benefits of seeking feedback, analyzing performance metrics, and incorporating lessons learned into future selling strategies. Readers gain insights into cultivating a growth mindset and continuously improving their skills and knowledge.

By the end of Chapter 29, readers have gained a comprehensive understanding of mastering the art of online auctions and marketplaces. They have explored the dynamics of online auctions, learned strategies for successful bidding and selling, leveraged effective listing techniques, optimized pricing and product descriptions, managed customer interactions, and expanded their reach through multiple platforms. Armed with this knowledge, readers can embark on their journey to become proficient in online auctions and marketplaces, maximizing their profits and establishing a successful e-commerce presence.

CHAPTER 30: DIVING INTO THE WORLD OF ONLINE REAL ESTATE

Chapter 30 delves into the world of online real estate, providing readers with a comprehensive understanding of how to navigate and capitalize on opportunities in the digital real estate marketplace. By exploring the dynamics of online real estate, understanding the benefits of virtual property transactions, conducting effective property research, leveraging online platforms, negotiating deals, and managing due diligence, readers can enter the realm of online real estate with confidence and maximize their investment potential.

30.1 Introduction to Online Real Estate: This section introduces the concept of online real estate and highlights its significance in the modern real estate landscape. It explores the benefits and opportunities presented by virtual property transactions and online real estate platforms. Readers gain insights into the potential of online real estate for buying, selling, or investing in properties.

30.2 Dynamics of Online Real Estate: Understanding the dynamics of online real estate is crucial for successful transactions. This section explores the unique aspects of the digital real estate marketplace, including virtual property listings, remote property viewing options, and the use of technology in property transactions. It discusses the advantages of online real estate, such as broader market access, convenience, and efficiency. Readers gain insights into the dynamics that shape the online real estate ecosystem.

30.3 Benefits of Virtual Property Transactions: Virtual property transactions offer several benefits to buyers, sellers, and investors. This section explores the advantages of virtual property transactions, including the ability to browse and research properties from anywhere, access to comprehensive property information, virtual property tours, and streamlined documentation processes. It discusses how virtual transactions save time, reduce costs, and facilitate global property transactions. Readers gain insights into the benefits of engaging in online real estate transactions.

30.4 Effective Property Research: Conducting thorough property research is essential for making informed investment decisions in online real estate. This section explores strategies for effective property research, such as utilizing online real estate databases, analyzing market trends, evaluating property valuations, and assessing neighborhood data. It discusses techniques for conducting due diligence on properties, including verifying property details, researching zoning regulations, and analyzing comparable property sales. Readers gain insights into conducting comprehensive property research in the online realm.

30.5 Leveraging Online Real Estate Platforms: Online real estate platforms play a significant role in facilitating property transactions. This section explores the various online platforms available for buying, selling, or investing in real estate, such as real estate marketplaces, listing websites, and crowdfunding platforms. It discusses the features and benefits of these platforms, including property search filters, interactive property listings, user reviews, and investor networking opportunities. Readers gain insights into leveraging online real estate platforms effectively.

30.6 Analyzing Property Listings: Analyzing property listings is crucial for identifying investment opportunities in online real estate. This section explores techniques for analyzing property listings, including evaluating property descriptions, assessing property images and videos, and examining property specifications and features. It discusses strategies for understanding property pricing, identifying value-add opportunities, and spotting potential red flags. Readers gain insights into analyzing property listings to make informed investment decisions.

30.7 Negotiating Deals: Negotiating deals effectively is vital for securing favorable terms in online real estate transactions. This section explores strategies for negotiating property deals, including understanding market conditions, researching property values, and setting realistic expectations. It discusses techniques for making competitive offers, negotiating price and terms, and conducting counteroffers. Readers gain insights into honing their negotiation skills in the online real estate arena.

30.8 Managing Due Diligence: Managing due diligence is crucial for mitigating risks and ensuring a successful online real estate transaction. This section explores the due diligence process, including verifying property ownership, assessing property condition, reviewing legal documents, and conducting inspections. It discusses techniques for engaging professionals, such as real estate agents, inspectors, and attorneys, to assist in the due diligence process. Readers gain insights into managing due diligence effectively in the online real estate realm.

30.9 Financing Options for Online Real Estate: Understanding financing options is important for facilitating online real estate transactions. This section explores financing options available for online real estate, such as traditional mortgages, peer-to-peer lending platforms, and crowdfunding. It discusses the requirements, benefits, and risks associated with each financing option. Readers gain insights into exploring financing options that align with their investment goals in the online real estate market.

30.10 Legal and Regulatory Considerations: Navigating legal and regulatory considerations is crucial when engaging in online real estate transactions. This section explores key legal and regulatory considerations, such as property ownership laws, contract requirements, and disclosure obligations. It discusses the importance of engaging legal professionals, understanding local regulations, and ensuring compliance throughout the transaction process. Readers gain insights into managing legal and regulatory aspects in online real estate transactions.

30.11 Managing Property Transactions and Closings: Managing property transactions and closings effectively is essential for a seamless online real estate experience. This section explores the transaction process, including making offers, negotiating contracts, conducting inspections, and coordinating property closings. It discusses strategies for organizing documentation, coordinating with various parties involved, and ensuring a smooth transition of ownership. Readers gain insights into managing property transactions and closings in the online real estate realm.

30.12 Staying Informed and Adapting to Market Trends: Staying informed and adapting to market trends is crucial for success in online real estate. This section emphasizes the importance of staying updated with market conditions, emerging trends, and regulatory changes. It discusses strategies for monitoring property values, analyzing market data, and adjusting investment strategies accordingly. Readers gain insights into staying informed and remaining agile in the dynamic online real estate market.

By the end of Chapter 30, readers have gained a comprehensive understanding of diving into the world of online real estate. They have explored the dynamics of online real estate, understood the benefits of virtual property transactions, learned strategies for effective property research, leveraged online real estate platforms, negotiated deals, managed due diligence, and navigated legal considerations. Armed with this knowledge, readers can confidently navigate the online real estate marketplace and capitalize on investment opportunities.

CHAPTER 31: MAXIMIZING RETURNS WITH PEER-TO-PEER LENDING

Chapter 31 explores the world of peer-to-peer lending, providing readers with a comprehensive understanding of how to maximize returns through this alternative investment strategy. By diving into the dynamics of peer-to-peer lending, understanding the benefits and risks, conducting effective borrower analysis, diversifying loan portfolios, and implementing risk management strategies, readers can capitalize on the potential of peer-to-peer lending to generate attractive returns.

31.1 Introduction to Peer-to-Peer Lending: This section introduces the concept of peer-to-peer lending and highlights its significance as an alternative investment opportunity. It explores the fundamental principles of peer-to-peer lending, where individuals lend money directly to borrowers through online platforms. Readers gain insights into the potential benefits and returns associated with peer-to-peer lending.

31.2 Dynamics of Peer-to-Peer Lending: Understanding the dynamics of peer-to-peer lending is essential for successful investment outcomes. This section explores the underlying mechanics of peer-to-peer lending platforms, including the process of loan origination, borrower evaluation, interest rate determination, and loan repayment. It discusses the role of technology in facilitating peer-to-peer lending transactions and connecting lenders with borrowers. Readers gain insights into the dynamics that shape the peer-to-peer lending landscape.

31.3 Benefits and Risks of Peer-to-Peer Lending: Peer-to-peer lending offers several benefits and risks that investors need to consider. This section explores the benefits of peer-to-peer lending, such as attractive interest rates, portfolio diversification, and potential higher returns compared to traditional fixed-income investments. It also discusses the risks associated with peer-to-peer lending, including borrower default, platform risk, and illiquidity. Readers gain insights into the potential rewards and risks of engaging in peer-to-peer lending.

31.4 Conducting Effective Borrower Analysis: Conducting thorough borrower analysis is crucial for mitigating risks and maximizing returns in peer-to-peer lending. This section explores strategies for evaluating borrower profiles, including assessing creditworthiness, analyzing income stability, and reviewing debt-to-income ratios. It discusses techniques for utilizing borrower credit reports, employment verification, and financial statements to assess the likelihood of loan repayment. Readers gain insights into effective borrower analysis in the peer-to-peer lending space.

31.5 Diversifying Loan Portfolios: Diversifying loan portfolios is a key risk management strategy in peer-to-peer lending. This section explores the benefits of diversification and its impact on reducing investment risk. It discusses techniques for diversifying loan portfolios by spreading investments across various borrower profiles, loan terms, and risk categories. It also explores the concept of fractional investing, where investors can fund multiple loans with smaller amounts. Readers gain insights into optimizing their loan portfolios through diversification.

31.6 Understanding Loan Risk and Return Profiles: Understanding loan risk and return profiles is crucial for making informed investment decisions in peer-to-peer lending. This section explores the different risk and return profiles associated with various types of loans, such as consumer loans, small business loans, or real estate loans. It discusses the factors that influence loan performance, including interest rates, loan terms, borrower creditworthiness, and economic conditions. Readers gain insights into assessing loan risk and return potential in peer-to-peer lending.

31.7 Implementing Risk Management Strategies: Implementing risk management strategies is essential for protecting investments in peer-to-peer lending. This section explores risk mitigation techniques, such as setting investment limits, diversifying across loan grades, and monitoring loan performance. It discusses the importance of establishing risk tolerance levels, conducting regular portfolio reviews, and adjusting investment strategies based on market conditions. Readers gain insights into implementing effective risk management strategies in peer-to-peer lending.

31.8 Leveraging Auto-Invest Tools and Features: Auto-invest tools and features offered by peer-to-peer lending platforms can enhance efficiency and streamline investment processes. This section explores the benefits of using auto-invest tools, which automatically allocate funds to loans based on predefined criteria. It discusses techniques for setting investment preferences, selecting loan parameters, and utilizing portfolio rebalancing features. Readers gain insights into leveraging auto-invest tools to optimize their peer-to-peer lending investments.

31.9 Monitoring Loan Performance: Monitoring loan performance is crucial for proactive risk management and decision-making in peer-to-peer lending. This section explores techniques for monitoring loan performance, including tracking repayment schedules, assessing borrower behavior, and identifying early warning signs of potential defaults. It discusses the importance of utilizing platform-provided data and analytics to evaluate loan performance and make informed investment decisions. Readers gain insights into effectively monitoring loan performance in peer-to-peer lending.

31.10 Reinvesting and Compounding Returns: Reinvesting and compounding returns can accelerate wealth accumulation in peer-to-peer lending. This section explores the benefits of reinvesting earned interest and principal repayments into new loans. It discusses techniques for reinvesting funds, optimizing reinvestment strategies, and utilizing compounding to maximize returns over time. Readers gain insights into the power of reinvesting and compounding returns in peer-to-peer lending.

31.11 Staying Informed and Adapting to Market Conditions: Staying informed and adapting to market conditions is crucial for successful peer-to-peer lending investments. This section emphasizes the importance of staying updated with platform developments, industry trends, and regulatory changes. It discusses strategies for monitoring economic indicators, interest rate movements, and borrower credit trends. Readers gain insights into staying informed and adjusting investment strategies based on changing market conditions.

31.12 Evaluating Secondary Market Opportunities: Some peer-to-peer lending platforms offer secondary marketplaces where investors can buy and sell existing loans. This section explores the benefits and risks of participating in secondary markets. It discusses techniques for evaluating secondary market opportunities, including analyzing loan listings, assessing loan prices, and understanding market liquidity. Readers gain insights into utilizing secondary markets to optimize their peer-to-peer lending portfolios.

By the end of Chapter 31, readers have gained a comprehensive understanding of maximizing returns with peer-to-peer lending. They have explored the dynamics of peer-to-peer lending, understood the benefits and risks, learned strategies for effective borrower analysis, diversified loan portfolios, implemented risk management strategies, and optimized their investments through reinvestment and compounding. Armed with this knowledge, readers can confidently navigate the peer-to-peer lending landscape and leverage this alternative investment avenue to maximize their returns.

CHAPTER 32: EXPLORING THE GIG ECONOMY AND TASK-BASED PLATFORMS

Chapter 32 delves into the world of the gig economy and task-based platforms, providing readers with a comprehensive understanding of this evolving work landscape. By exploring the dynamics of the gig economy, understanding the benefits and challenges of gig work, navigating task-based platforms, building a successful gig career, and managing the gig work-life balance, readers can embrace the opportunities and make informed decisions in this rapidly growing sector.

32.1 Introduction to the Gig Economy: This section introduces the concept of the gig economy and highlights its significance in the modern workforce. It explores the transformation of traditional employment models and the rise of flexible, short-term, and task-based work arrangements. Readers gain insights into the growth and impact of the gig economy on individuals and the overall economy.

32.2 Dynamics of the Gig Economy: Understanding the dynamics of the gig economy is crucial for navigating the gig work landscape. This section explores the underlying mechanics of the gig economy, including the role of digital platforms, the gig worker-client relationship, and the gig worker's autonomy. It discusses the advantages of flexibility, freedom, and diversification of income streams in gig work. Readers gain insights into the dynamics that shape the gig economy.

32.3 Benefits of Gig Work: Gig work offers several benefits to individuals seeking flexible employment opportunities. This section explores the advantages of gig work, including the ability to choose projects, work on one's own terms, and experience a variety of tasks and industries. It discusses the potential for higher income, personal growth, and work-life balance in gig work. Readers gain insights into the benefits associated with participating in the gig economy.

32.4 Challenges of Gig Work: While gig work offers benefits, it also presents challenges that individuals need to consider. This section explores the challenges of gig work, such as income volatility, lack of benefits and job security, and the need for self-promotion and business management skills. It discusses strategies for mitigating these challenges, such as financial planning, building a strong professional network, and investing in professional development. Readers gain insights into the potential obstacles and how to overcome them in gig work.

32.5 Navigating Task-Based Platforms: Task-based platforms play a significant role in connecting gig workers with clients and facilitating gig work assignments. This section explores popular task-based platforms across various industries, such as ride-hailing, food delivery, freelance writing, graphic design, and virtual assistance. It discusses the features, requirements, and earning potential of these platforms. Readers gain insights into navigating task-based platforms and finding suitable gig work opportunities.

32.6 Building a Successful Gig Career: Building a successful gig career requires strategic planning and execution. This section explores strategies for establishing a strong gig career, including identifying marketable skills, building a personal brand, and leveraging online platforms and social media for self-promotion. It discusses techniques for networking, cultivating client relationships, and seeking positive reviews and referrals. Readers gain insights into building a successful gig career in the gig economy.

32.7 Managing Gig Work-Life Balance: Managing work-life balance is crucial for gig workers who often juggle multiple projects and clients. This section explores strategies for maintaining a healthy work-life balance, such as setting boundaries, managing time effectively, and prioritizing self-care. It discusses techniques for managing workloads, avoiding burnout, and fostering work-life integration. Readers gain insights into maintaining a sustainable work-life balance in the gig economy.

32.8 Developing Professional Skills: Continuously developing professional skills is essential for gig workers to stay competitive and thrive in the gig economy. This section explores strategies for ongoing skill development, including online courses, certifications, workshops, and networking events. It discusses the importance of staying updated with industry trends and acquiring new skills to meet client demands. Readers gain insights into nurturing professional growth and staying relevant in the gig economy.

32.9 Financial Planning and Tax Considerations: Financial planning and tax considerations are important aspects of gig work. This section explores strategies for effective financial management, including budgeting, saving for taxes, and managing irregular income. It discusses tax obligations and considerations for gig workers, such as self-employment taxes, deductible expenses, and record-keeping practices. Readers gain insights into optimizing their financial planning and complying with tax requirements in gig work.

32.10 Collaborative Opportunities in the Gig Economy: Collaborative opportunities in the gig economy enable gig workers to collaborate with others and take on larger projects. This section explores collaborative models, such as forming gig worker collectives, joining freelancer communities, and partnering with other professionals. It discusses the benefits of collaboration, such as knowledge sharing, increased project scope, and enhanced client offerings. Readers gain insights into leveraging collaborative opportunities in the gig economy.

32.11 Adapting to Technological Advancements: Adapting to technological advancements is crucial for gig workers to stay relevant and competitive. This section explores emerging technologies that impact the gig economy, such as artificial intelligence, automation, and blockchain. It discusses the potential opportunities and challenges associated with these advancements and emphasizes the importance of continuous learning and adaptability. Readers gain insights into embracing technological advancements and leveraging them in the gig economy.

32.12 Ethical Considerations in the Gig Economy: Ethical considerations play a significant role in gig work. This section explores ethical issues and dilemmas that gig workers may encounter, such as fair compensation, privacy concerns, and responsible use of customer data. It discusses strategies for maintaining ethical standards, including transparent communication, respecting client confidentiality, and adhering to professional codes of conduct. Readers gain insights into navigating ethical considerations in the gig economy.

By the end of Chapter 32, readers have gained a comprehensive understanding of exploring the gig economy and task-based platforms. They have explored the dynamics of the gig economy, understood the benefits and challenges of gig work, learned strategies for navigating task-based platforms, building a successful gig career, and managing the gig work-life balance. Armed with this knowledge, readers can confidently navigate the gig economy, make informed decisions, and thrive in the rapidly evolving world of gig work.

CHAPTER 33: MONETIZING YOUR PHOTOGRAPHY SKILLS ONLINE

Chapter 33 explores the opportunities for photographers to monetize their skills in the digital era. With the rise of online platforms and the increasing demand for visual content, photographers can leverage the internet to showcase their work, reach a global audience, and generate income. This chapter provides a comprehensive guide on how photographers can monetize their photography skills online through various avenues such as stock photography, selling prints, offering photography services, creating online courses, and more.

33.1 Introduction to Monetizing Photography Skills Online: This section introduces the concept of monetizing photography skills online and highlights the potential for photographers to showcase their work and generate income through digital platforms. It explores the changing landscape of the photography industry in the digital era and the opportunities that arise from the widespread use of visual content online. Readers gain insights into the vast potential for photographers to monetize their skills through various online avenues.

33.2 Showcasing and Licensing Photos on Stock Photography Platforms: Stock photography platforms provide photographers with an opportunity to monetize their work by licensing their photos to individuals and businesses worldwide. This section explores the process of showcasing and licensing photos on stock photography platforms. It discusses techniques for curating a strong portfolio, understanding licensing agreements, optimizing metadata and keywords, and meeting the specific requirements of stock photography platforms.

Readers gain insights into maximizing their earnings through stock photography.

33.3 Selling Prints and Artwork Online: Selling prints and artwork online is another avenue for photographers to monetize their skills and creativity. This section explores strategies for selling prints and artwork through dedicated online marketplaces, personal websites, or print-on-demand services. It discusses considerations such as print quality, pricing strategies, packaging, and shipping logistics. It also explores options for offering limited edition prints or customized artwork to cater to specific customer preferences. Readers gain insights into successfully selling their photography as physical products.

33.4 Offering Photography Services: Photographers can monetize their skills by offering photography services to clients. This section explores various photography services that can be provided online, such as event photography, portrait sessions, product photography, and more. It discusses strategies for marketing photography services through personal websites, social media platforms, and online directories. It also explores pricing considerations, client communication, and delivering high-quality services. Readers gain insights into building a successful photography service business online.

33.5 Creating Online Photography Courses and Workshops: Creating and selling online photography courses and workshops is an excellent way for photographers to share their expertise and generate income. This section explores the process of creating and marketing online photography courses and workshops. It discusses techniques for identifying target audiences, defining course content and structure, selecting appropriate online platforms, and effectively promoting courses through various marketing channels. Readers gain insights into leveraging their knowledge and skills to create educational products.

33.6 Participating in Photography Contests and Grants: Participating in photography contests and applying for grants can provide photographers with both financial rewards and valuable exposure. This section explores strategies for finding reputable photography contests and grants, understanding submission guidelines, and preparing compelling entries. It discusses the benefits of participating in these opportunities, such as recognition, networking, and potential financial support. Readers gain insights into leveraging contests and grants to advance their photography careers and generate income.

33.7 Collaborating with Brands and Influencers: Collaborating with brands and influencers is a growing trend in the photography industry. This section explores the potential for photographers to collaborate with brands for commercial projects or partner with influencers for sponsored content creation. It discusses strategies for identifying suitable brand partnerships, negotiating contracts and licensing agreements, and ensuring a mutually beneficial collaboration. Readers gain insights into capitalizing on brand collaborations and influencer partnerships to monetize their photography skills.

33.8 Building an Online Presence and Brand: Building a strong online presence and brand is crucial for photographers looking to monetize their skills effectively. This section explores strategies for creating a compelling online portfolio, optimizing websites for search engines, and establishing a consistent brand identity. It discusses techniques for leveraging social media platforms, engaging with online communities, and utilizing digital marketing strategies to attract clients and customers. Readers gain insights into building an influential online presence as a photographer.

33.9 Leveraging Social Media Platforms for Exposure and Sales: Social media platforms offer photographers an opportunity to reach a wide audience, gain exposure, and drive sales. This section explores strategies for leveraging popular social media platforms such as Instagram, Facebook, and Pinterest. It discusses techniques for creating visually appealing content, engaging with followers, utilizing hashtags and analytics, and driving traffic to online portfolios or e-commerce platforms. Readers gain insights into effectively utilizing social media to monetize their photography skills.

33.10 Collaborating with Online Publications and Blogs: Collaborating with online publications and blogs can provide photographers with exposure and potential income opportunities. This section explores strategies for identifying relevant online publications and blogs, pitching photography features or photo essays, and negotiating compensation or licensing terms. It discusses the benefits of such collaborations, including increased visibility, credibility, and potential for future commissions. Readers gain insights into leveraging online publications and blogs to monetize their photography skills.

33.11 Expanding into Video and Multimedia: Expanding into video and multimedia content creation can broaden the revenue streams for photographers. This section explores the potential of video production, vlogging, creating visual storytelling projects, or offering multimedia services. It discusses the equipment and skills needed for multimedia production, as well as strategies for marketing and monetizing video content online. Readers gain insights into diversifying their offerings and exploring new opportunities in the digital content landscape.

33.12 Continuous Learning and Adaptation: Continuous learning and adaptation are essential for photographers aiming to succeed in monetizing their skills online. This section emphasizes the importance of staying updated with industry trends, learning new techniques, and embracing technological advancements. It discusses resources for ongoing education, networking opportunities, and the benefits of embracing change and innovation. Readers gain insights into cultivating a growth mindset and continuously evolving their photography skills and business strategies.

By the end of Chapter 33, readers have gained a comprehensive understanding of monetizing their photography skills online. They have explored various avenues such as stock photography, selling prints, offering photography services, creating online courses, and collaborating with brands or influencers. Armed with this knowledge, photographers can confidently navigate the online photography landscape, showcase their work, and generate income through their passion and skills.

CHAPTER 34: UNLEASHING THE POWER OF ONLINE TUTORING AND EDUCATION

Chapter 34 explores the vast potential of online tutoring and education, providing readers with a comprehensive understanding of how to unleash the power of digital platforms to deliver educational services, connect with learners worldwide, and create impactful learning experiences. By delving into the dynamics of online tutoring and education, understanding the benefits and challenges, exploring various online teaching platforms and tools, and implementing effective teaching strategies, readers can tap into the growing demand for online learning and make a positive impact in the education space.

34.1 Introduction to Online Tutoring and Education: This section introduces the concept of online tutoring and education and highlights its significance in the digital age. It explores the transformative impact of technology on the education landscape, leading to the emergence of online tutoring platforms and the increased accessibility of educational resources. Readers gain insights into the potential of online tutoring and education to overcome geographical barriers, enhance personalized learning, and reach learners globally.

34.2 Dynamics of Online Tutoring and Education: Understanding the dynamics of online tutoring and education is crucial for effectively engaging with learners in the digital realm. This section explores the underlying mechanics of online tutoring platforms, virtual classrooms, and learning management systems. It discusses the advantages of real-time communication, interactive learning tools, and personalized learning experiences. Readers gain insights into the dynamics that shape the online tutoring and education landscape.

34.3 Benefits of Online Tutoring and Education: Online tutoring and education offer numerous benefits to both educators and learners. This section explores the advantages of online tutoring and education, including flexible scheduling, individualized instruction, access to a wide range of educational resources, and the ability to reach diverse learners worldwide. It discusses the potential for personalized feedback, collaborative learning, and enhanced engagement in online learning environments. Readers gain insights into the benefits associated with engaging in online tutoring and education.

34.4 Challenges in Online Tutoring and Education: While online tutoring and education present various advantages, they also come with unique challenges. This section explores the challenges educators may face, such as technological barriers, connectivity issues, maintaining learner motivation, and adapting instructional strategies for virtual environments. It discusses strategies for overcoming these challenges, including familiarizing oneself with online teaching tools, creating engaging learning experiences, and providing effective support to learners. Readers gain insights into navigating and mitigating challenges in online tutoring and education.

34.5 Online Tutoring Platforms and Tools: Online tutoring platforms and tools play a crucial role in facilitating online tutoring and education. This section explores popular online tutoring platforms, virtual classrooms, and video conferencing tools. It discusses their features, functionalities, and suitability for different teaching contexts. It also explores supplementary tools for interactive whiteboarding, document sharing, and collaborative learning. Readers gain insights into selecting and utilizing appropriate online tutoring platforms and tools.

34.6 Designing Engaging Online Learning Experiences: Designing engaging online learning experiences is essential for capturing learners' attention and fostering effective learning outcomes. This section explores strategies for creating interactive and dynamic online lessons, incorporating multimedia elements, and utilizing gamification techniques. It discusses techniques for promoting learner engagement, providing opportunities for active participation, and facilitating peer collaboration in virtual classrooms. Readers gain insights into designing impactful online learning experiences.

34.7 Personalizing Instruction in Online Tutoring: Personalizing instruction is a key factor in the success of online tutoring. This section explores strategies for tailoring instruction to meet individual learner needs, such as conducting learner assessments, setting learning goals, and designing customized learning paths. It discusses techniques for providing targeted feedback, tracking learner progress, and adapting instructional strategies to optimize learning outcomes. Readers gain insights into personalizing instruction in online tutoring to enhance learner engagement and achievement.

34.8 Leveraging Data and Analytics in Online Education: Data and analytics play a significant role in optimizing online education experiences. This section explores the use of data and analytics to track learner performance, identify learning gaps, and provide personalized recommendations. It discusses the importance of data privacy and ethical considerations in handling learner data. It also explores the potential of learning analytics to inform instructional decision-making and improve learning outcomes. Readers gain insights into leveraging data and analytics in online education.

34.9 Expanding Reach through Online Course Creation: Creating and selling online courses is an effective way for educators to reach a broader audience and monetize their expertise. This section explores the process of creating online courses, including defining learning objectives, structuring course content, and utilizing multimedia elements. It discusses strategies for marketing and promoting online courses through websites, social media, and online learning platforms. Readers gain insights into expanding their reach and impact through online course creation.

34.10 Supporting Student Engagement and Motivation: Supporting student engagement and motivation is crucial for successful online tutoring and education. This section explores strategies for fostering learner motivation, promoting active participation, and building a supportive online learning community. It discusses techniques for providing timely and constructive feedback, incorporating learner interests and preferences, and utilizing motivational strategies such as goal setting and rewards. Readers gain insights into supporting student engagement and motivation in online learning environments.

34.11 Assessing Learning Outcomes in Online Education: Assessing learning outcomes is an integral part of online education. This section explores strategies for designing formative and summative assessments that align with learning objectives and instructional strategies. It discusses techniques for utilizing online assessment tools, providing timely feedback, and promoting self-assessment and reflection. It also explores strategies for authentic assessment, such as project-based assessments or collaborative assignments. Readers gain insights into assessing learning outcomes effectively in online education.

34.12 Professional Development and Continuous Learning: Professional development and continuous learning are essential for educators in the online tutoring and education space. This section emphasizes the importance of staying updated with educational trends, technological advancements, and research in online pedagogy. It discusses resources for ongoing professional development, such as webinars, conferences, online communities, and educational publications. Readers gain insights into cultivating a growth mindset and continuously improving their online tutoring and teaching practices.

By the end of Chapter 34, readers have gained a comprehensive understanding of unleashing the power of online tutoring and education. They have explored the dynamics of online tutoring and education, understood the benefits and challenges, learned about online tutoring platforms and tools, implemented effective teaching strategies, and embraced continuous professional development. Armed with this knowledge, educators can confidently harness the potential of online tutoring and education to deliver impactful learning experiences and empower learners in the digital era.

CHAPTER 35: MAKING MONEY WITH VIRTUAL EVENTS AND WEBINARS

Chapter 35 explores the exciting opportunities for making money through virtual events and webinars. With the increasing popularity of online gatherings and digital conferences, individuals and businesses can leverage virtual platforms to host events, deliver educational content, and generate revenue. This chapter provides a comprehensive guide on how to monetize virtual events and webinars by understanding audience needs, creating compelling content, utilizing effective marketing strategies, exploring monetization options, and delivering exceptional online experiences.

35.1 Introduction to Virtual Events and Webinars: This section introduces the concept of virtual events and webinars and highlights their significance in the digital age. It explores the transformative impact of technology on event hosting and knowledge sharing, leading to the rise of virtual platforms and the increasing accessibility of online events. Readers gain insights into the potential of virtual events and webinars to reach a global audience, deliver engaging content, and generate revenue.

35.2 Understanding Audience Needs and Trends: Understanding audience needs and staying updated with trends is essential for creating successful virtual events and webinars. This section explores techniques for identifying target audiences, conducting market research, and gathering insights into audience preferences and expectations. It discusses trends in virtual event formats, content delivery methods, and interactive features. Readers gain insights into aligning their offerings with audience needs and capitalizing on emerging trends.

35.3 Creating Compelling Webinar and Event Content: Creating compelling content is crucial for attracting and engaging audiences in virtual events and webinars. This section explores strategies for designing captivating presentations, structuring content for maximum impact, and incorporating interactive elements such as polls, quizzes, and Q&A sessions. It discusses techniques for delivering informative and entertaining sessions, leveraging storytelling techniques, and utilizing multimedia resources. Readers gain insights into creating high-quality content that resonates with virtual event attendees.

35.4 Leveraging Virtual Event Platforms and Tools: Virtual event platforms and tools play a crucial role in hosting successful virtual events and webinars. This section explores popular virtual event platforms, webinar hosting platforms, and associated tools for seamless event management, content delivery, and audience engagement. It discusses features such as registration management, live streaming, chat functions, and audience analytics. Readers gain insights into selecting and utilizing appropriate virtual event platforms and tools.

35.5 Marketing and Promoting Virtual Events and Webinars: Effective marketing and promotion are essential for driving attendance and revenue in virtual events and webinars. This section explores strategies for creating compelling event landing pages, utilizing social media and email marketing, leveraging influencers and partnerships, and utilizing paid advertising. It discusses techniques for generating buzz, building anticipation, and targeting specific audience segments. Readers gain insights into maximizing event visibility and attracting a diverse audience.

35.6 Monetization Options for Virtual Events and Webinars: There are various monetization options available for virtual events and webinars. This section explores different revenue models, including ticket sales, sponsorships, exhibitor booths, premium content access, and pay-per-view models. It discusses pricing strategies, tiered ticketing options, and negotiating sponsorships and partnerships. It also explores opportunities for upselling and cross-selling additional products or services. Readers gain insights into monetizing their virtual events and webinars effectively.

35.7 Designing Sponsorship and Partnership Programs: Sponsorships and partnerships can play a significant role in monetizing virtual events and webinars. This section explores strategies for designing sponsorship and partnership programs, including identifying potential sponsors, defining sponsorship packages, and demonstrating the value proposition for sponsors. It discusses techniques for building relationships, offering promotional opportunities, and delivering sponsor benefits. Readers gain insights into leveraging sponsorships and partnerships to enhance revenue streams.

35.8 Providing Value-Added Services and Upselling Opportunities: Providing value-added services and upselling opportunities can increase revenue potential in virtual events and webinars. This section explores strategies for offering additional services such as post-event recordings, exclusive resources, or networking opportunities. It discusses techniques for upselling premium packages, VIP access, or consulting services. It also explores options for offering merchandise, books, or courses as complementary products. Readers gain insights into maximizing revenue through value-added services and upselling.

35.9 Ensuring a Seamless Online Experience: Delivering a seamless online experience is crucial for the success of virtual events and webinars. This section explores techniques for ensuring technical stability, optimizing video and audio quality, and providing reliable customer support. It discusses best practices for managing online interactions, moderating discussions, and troubleshooting common issues. It also explores accessibility considerations, such as providing closed captions or translation services. Readers gain insights into delivering exceptional online experiences.

35.10 Gathering and Analyzing Attendee Data: Gathering and analyzing attendee data can provide valuable insights for improving future virtual events and webinars. This section explores techniques for collecting attendee data, such as registration information, engagement metrics, or post-event surveys. It discusses the importance of data privacy and ethical considerations in handling attendee data. It also explores ways to analyze data to identify audience preferences, measure event success, and make data-driven decisions. Readers gain insights into leveraging attendee data for continuous improvement.

35.11 Leveraging Post-Event Opportunities: Post-event opportunities can contribute to sustained revenue generation and long-term audience engagement. This section explores strategies for leveraging post-event opportunities, such as repurposing event content for on-demand access, creating post-event follow-up resources, or offering exclusive discounts for future events. It discusses techniques for nurturing relationships with attendees, encouraging feedback and testimonials, and maintaining communication channels for ongoing engagement. Readers gain insights into maximizing post-event opportunities.

35.12 Continuous Learning and Adaptation: Continuous learning and adaptation are essential for success in the world of virtual events and webinars. This section emphasizes the importance of staying updated with technological advancements, industry trends, and evolving audience preferences. It discusses resources for ongoing professional development, attending virtual conferences, joining industry communities, and embracing innovation. Readers gain insights into cultivating a growth mindset and continuously improving their virtual event and webinar strategies.

By the end of Chapter 35, readers have gained a comprehensive understanding of making money with virtual events and webinars. They have explored the dynamics of virtual events and webinars, understood audience needs and trends, learned strategies for creating compelling content, marketing and monetizing virtual events, and delivering exceptional online experiences. Armed with this knowledge, event organizers and content creators can confidently tap into the opportunities of virtual events and webinars, generate revenue, and deliver impactful experiences in the digital realm.

CHAPTER 36: EXPANDING YOUR REACH WITH ONLINE PR AND CONTENT MARKETING

Chapter 36 explores the power of online PR (Public Relations) and content marketing in expanding reach and building a strong online presence. In today's digital world, businesses and individuals can leverage online platforms to effectively promote their brand, reach a broader audience, and establish themselves as industry leaders. This chapter provides a comprehensive guide on how to utilize online PR and content marketing strategies to enhance visibility, attract customers, and cultivate a loyal following.

36.1 Introduction to Online PR and Content Marketing: This section introduces the concept of online PR and content marketing and highlights their significance in the digital age. It explores the transformative impact of technology on the field of public relations, leading to the rise of online platforms for brand promotion and reputation management. Readers gain insights into the potential of online PR and content marketing to create brand awareness, establish credibility, and engage with target audiences.

36.2 Building a Strong Online Presence: Building a strong online presence is essential for success in the digital realm. This section explores strategies for creating a compelling brand identity, optimizing websites for search engines, and establishing a consistent online voice and image. It discusses techniques for leveraging social media platforms, online directories, and review sites to enhance online visibility and reputation. Readers gain insights into building a strong foundation for online PR and content marketing efforts.

36.3 Crafting Engaging and Valuable Content: Crafting engaging and valuable content is at the core of successful online PR and content marketing. This section explores strategies for identifying target audiences, understanding their needs and interests, and creating content that resonates with them. It discusses techniques for developing compelling blog posts, articles, videos, infographics, and podcasts. It also explores the importance of storytelling, authenticity, and providing value to readers. Readers gain insights into creating high-quality content that captures attention and drives engagement.

36.4 Leveraging SEO (Search Engine Optimization): Leveraging SEO is crucial for improving online visibility and driving organic traffic to your content. This section explores strategies for conducting keyword research, optimizing website and content structure, and utilizing on-page and off-page SEO techniques. It discusses the importance of metadata, URL structure, mobile optimization, and link building. It also explores the role of SEO in content promotion and driving conversions. Readers gain insights into maximizing their content's discoverability through effective SEO practices.

36.5 Building Relationships with Influencers and Media: Building relationships with influencers and media professionals can significantly amplify your online PR efforts. This section explores strategies for identifying relevant influencers and media outlets, engaging with them, and seeking collaboration opportunities. It discusses techniques for reaching out to influencers and media professionals, such as personalized pitches, offering exclusive content, or providing expert insights. Readers gain insights into leveraging influencer and media partnerships for increased brand exposure and credibility.

36.6 Engaging with Online Communities and Forums: Engaging with online communities and forums allows you to connect with your target audience, establish thought leadership, and drive brand awareness. This section explores strategies for identifying relevant online communities and forums, participating in discussions, and providing value through insightful contributions. It discusses techniques for building trust, offering helpful advice, and subtly promoting your brand within community guidelines. Readers gain insights into effectively engaging with online communities and forums.

36.7 Utilizing Social Media for PR and Content Promotion: Social media platforms are powerful tools for PR and content promotion. This section explores strategies for selecting the right social media platforms for your target audience, creating compelling profiles, and developing a social media content strategy. It discusses techniques for growing your social media following, engaging with followers, and utilizing paid advertising and influencer collaborations. It also explores social media analytics and measuring the effectiveness of your social media efforts. Readers gain insights into leveraging social media for maximum PR and content marketing impact.

36.8 Implementing Email Marketing Campaigns: Email marketing remains a highly effective tool for nurturing leads, building relationships, and driving conversions. This section explores strategies for building an email subscriber list, creating engaging email content, and optimizing email campaigns for maximum impact. It discusses techniques for segmentation, personalization, and automation to deliver targeted and relevant messages. It also explores email marketing analytics and measuring the success of your campaigns. Readers gain insights into implementing successful email marketing campaigns.

36.9 Harnessing the Power of Online Press Releases: Online press releases provide an effective way to distribute news and updates about your brand to a wide audience. This section explores strategies for writing compelling press releases, optimizing them for search engines and media distribution platforms, and targeting relevant media outlets. It discusses techniques for crafting attention-grabbing headlines, including multimedia elements, and incorporating SEO keywords. Readers gain insights into maximizing the impact of online press releases in their PR efforts.

36.10 Creating Thought Leadership Content: Establishing yourself as a thought leader in your industry can significantly enhance your online reputation and attract a loyal following. This section explores strategies for creating thought leadership content, such as whitepapers, research reports, case studies, and expert blog posts. It discusses techniques for providing unique insights, backing claims with data, and promoting your thought leadership content through social media and industry publications. Readers gain insights into becoming a recognized authority in their field.

36.11 Measuring PR and Content Marketing Success: Measuring the success of your PR and content marketing efforts is crucial for refining strategies and optimizing outcomes. This section explores key metrics and tools for tracking website traffic, engagement levels, social media reach, email open rates, and conversions. It discusses techniques for analyzing data, identifying trends, and making data-driven decisions. It also explores the importance of feedback and customer testimonials in gauging PR and content marketing success. Readers gain insights into effectively measuring and evaluating their PR and content marketing efforts.

36.12 Continuous Learning and Adaptation: Continuous learning and adaptation are essential in the fast-paced world of online PR and content marketing. This section emphasizes the importance of staying updated with industry trends, technological advancements, and evolving audience preferences. It discusses resources for ongoing professional development, such as industry conferences, webinars, online courses, and networking opportunities. Readers gain insights into cultivating a growth mindset and continuously improving their online PR and content marketing strategies.

By the end of Chapter 36, readers have gained a comprehensive

understanding of expanding their reach with online PR and content marketing. They have explored strategies for building a strong online presence, crafting compelling content, leveraging SEO and social media, engaging with influencers and communities, and measuring success. Armed with this knowledge, individuals and businesses can confidently harness the power of online PR and content marketing to expand their reach, build brand awareness, and achieve their business goals in the digital era.

CHAPTER 37: EXPLORING THE WORLD OF ONLINE FOREX TRADING

Chapter 37 delves into the exciting world of online Forex trading, providing readers with a comprehensive understanding of the foreign exchange market and the opportunities it presents for traders. Forex trading, or foreign exchange trading, involves the buying and selling of currencies with the aim of profiting from the fluctuations in exchange rates. This chapter serves as a guide, explaining the fundamentals of Forex trading, the key participants, the various trading strategies, risk management techniques, and the necessary tools and platforms for successful trading.

37.1 Introduction to Forex Trading: This section provides an introduction to Forex trading, highlighting its significance in the global financial market. It explains the basic concept of buying and selling currencies, the role of exchange rates, and the factors that influence currency movements. Readers gain insights into the size and liquidity of the Forex market, its decentralized nature, and the potential for profit in currency trading.

37.2 Understanding the Forex Market: Understanding the Forex market is crucial for successful trading. This section explores the structure of the Forex market, including the major currency pairs, currency crosses, and exotic currency pairs. It discusses the role of central banks, financial institutions, corporations, and retail traders in shaping market dynamics. Readers gain insights into the different trading sessions, market liquidity, and the impact of economic news and geopolitical events on currency prices.

37.3 Trading Basics: Currency Pairs and Quotes: Trading in the Forex market involves trading currency pairs. This section explains the concept of currency pairs, including base currency and quote currency, and how exchange rates are quoted. It discusses major currency pairs such as EUR/USD, USD/JPY, GBP/USD, and others, as well as minor and exotic currency pairs. Readers gain insights into interpreting currency quotes, understanding bid and ask prices, and calculating profits and losses.

37.4 Fundamental Analysis in Forex Trading: Fundamental analysis plays a crucial role in Forex trading by examining economic, political, and social factors that impact currency values. This section explores the key economic indicators, such as GDP, inflation rates, interest rates, and employment data, and their influence on currency movements. It discusses the importance of staying updated with global news and events and utilizing economic calendars and news feeds for fundamental analysis. Readers gain insights into integrating fundamental analysis into their trading strategies.

37.5 Technical Analysis in Forex Trading: Technical analysis is an essential tool for Forex traders, as it involves analyzing historical price data and patterns to predict future price movements. This section explores popular technical analysis tools and indicators, such as trend lines, support and resistance levels, moving averages, and oscillators. It discusses chart patterns, candlestick analysis, and the importance of timeframes in technical analysis. Readers gain insights into incorporating technical analysis into their trading decisions.

37.6 Trading Strategies in Forex: Various trading strategies can be employed in Forex trading, depending on traders' risk tolerance, time horizon, and market conditions. This section explores common trading strategies, including trend following, range trading, breakout trading, and carry trading. It discusses the use of indicators and chart patterns in strategy development. Readers gain insights into selecting and implementing suitable trading strategies based on their trading goals and market conditions.

37.7 Risk Management in Forex Trading: Effective risk management is crucial in Forex trading to protect capital and minimize losses. This section explores risk management techniques, including setting stop-loss orders, defining risk-reward ratios, and utilizing position sizing techniques. It discusses the importance of maintaining trading discipline, managing emotions, and avoiding excessive leverage. Readers gain insights into developing a comprehensive risk management plan and implementing it consistently.

37.8 Trading Psychology: Trading psychology plays a significant role in Forex trading, as emotions and biases can impact decision-making and trading outcomes. This section explores the psychological aspects of trading, including fear, greed, overtrading, and confirmation bias. It discusses techniques for managing emotions, maintaining objectivity, and developing a resilient mindset. Readers gain insights into cultivating the right trading psychology for success in Forex trading.

37.9 Choosing a Forex Broker: Selecting a reliable Forex broker is crucial for a trader's success. This section explores the factors to consider when choosing a Forex broker, including regulation, reputation, trading platforms, fees, spreads, and customer support. It discusses the importance of demo accounts for testing trading strategies and evaluating broker services. Readers gain insights into selecting a trustworthy broker that aligns with their trading needs.

37.10 Tools and Platforms for Forex Trading: Utilizing the right tools and trading platforms is essential in Forex trading. This section explores popular trading platforms, such as MetaTrader 4 (MT4) and MetaTrader 5 (MT5), and their features for charting, order execution, and analysis. It discusses additional tools and resources for market research, economic calendar tracking, and automated trading. Readers gain insights into leveraging technology to enhance their trading experience.

37.11 Backtesting and Demo Trading: Backtesting and demo trading are valuable practices for Forex traders to refine their strategies and gain experience without risking real money. This section explores the process of backtesting, which involves analyzing historical data to assess the performance of a trading strategy. It discusses the benefits of demo trading, where traders can practice trading with virtual funds in real market conditions. Readers gain insights into utilizing backtesting and demo trading to improve their trading skills.

37.12 Continuous Learning and Adaptation: Continuous learning and adaptation are essential in the dynamic Forex market. This section emphasizes the importance of staying updated with economic news, market trends, and evolving trading strategies. It discusses resources for ongoing education, such as Forex trading courses, webinars, books, and online communities. Readers gain insights into cultivating a growth mindset, continuously improving their trading skills, and adapting to changing market conditions.

By the end of Chapter 37, readers have gained a comprehensive understanding of exploring the world of online Forex trading. They have explored the fundamentals of Forex trading, understood the dynamics of the Forex market, learned trading strategies, risk management techniques, and the necessary tools and platforms. Armed with this knowledge, traders can confidently engage in Forex trading, make informed decisions, and potentially profit from the exciting world of currency trading.

CHAPTER 38: GENERATING INCOME THROUGH ONLINE GAMING AND ESPORTS

Chapter 38 delves into the exciting world of online gaming and esports, exploring the opportunities for generating income through these rapidly growing industries. With the rise of online gaming platforms, competitive esports leagues, and streaming platforms, individuals can now monetize their passion for gaming and participate in the thriving gaming economy. This chapter serves as a comprehensive guide, discussing various avenues for income generation, including esports competitions, game streaming, content creation, sponsorships, and merchandise sales.

38.1 Introduction to Online Gaming and Esports: This section provides an introduction to the world of online gaming and esports, highlighting their exponential growth and global popularity. It explores the evolution of gaming from recreational hobby to a professional industry, driven by advancements in technology and the emergence of competitive gaming leagues. Readers gain insights into the immense potential of online gaming and esports for income generation and career opportunities.

38.2 Understanding the Gaming Economy: Understanding the gaming economy is crucial for individuals looking to generate income through online gaming and esports. This section explores the various components of the gaming economy, including game sales, in-game purchases, virtual currency, and digital marketplaces. It discusses the impact of microtransactions, loot boxes, and game subscriptions on revenue generation. Readers gain insights into the monetization models that drive the gaming industry.

38.3 Participating in Esports Competitions: Esports competitions offer lucrative opportunities for skilled gamers to showcase their talent and earn income. This section explores the world of esports tournaments, ranging from grassroots events to international championships. It discusses popular esports games, team-based and individual competitions, and the competitive structure of esports leagues. Readers gain insights into the process of joining or forming esports teams, participating in tournaments, and earning prize money and sponsorships.

38.4 Game Streaming and Content Creation: Game streaming and content creation have revolutionized the way gamers engage with their audience and generate income. This section explores the concept of game streaming, where gamers broadcast their gameplay live over platforms like Twitch, YouTube, or Facebook Gaming. It discusses strategies for building a loyal fan base, creating engaging content, and monetizing streams through ad revenue, subscriptions, donations, and sponsorships. Readers gain insights into launching a successful streaming career.

38.5 Becoming a Gaming Influencer: Becoming a gaming influencer allows individuals to leverage their expertise and personality to build a dedicated following and monetize their influence. This section explores the world of gaming influencers, including streamers, YouTubers, and social media personalities. It discusses strategies for growing a gaming-focused social media presence, partnering with brands for sponsored content, and utilizing affiliate marketing. Readers gain insights into building a personal brand as a gaming influencer.

38.6 Sponsorships and Brand Partnerships: Sponsorships and brand partnerships offer significant income opportunities for gamers and content creators. This section explores the process of securing sponsorships, working with brands, and promoting products or services to an engaged audience. It discusses the importance of building relationships with brands, developing a professional media kit, and negotiating favorable sponsorship deals. Readers gain insights into leveraging their influence to secure lucrative partnerships.

38.7 Creating and Selling Gaming Merchandise: Creating and selling gaming merchandise allows gamers and content creators to monetize their brand and connect with their audience on a tangible level. This section explores the process of designing and producing gaming merchandise, including apparel, accessories, collectibles, and digital products. It discusses various sales channels, such as e-commerce platforms and gaming conventions. Readers gain insights into building a merchandise brand and generating income through product sales.

38.8 Game Development and Publishing: Game development and publishing offer opportunities for individuals with programming or creative skills to generate income in the gaming industry. This section explores the process of developing and publishing games, including designing gameplay mechanics, creating art assets, programming, and marketing. It discusses revenue models such as game sales, in-app purchases, and downloadable content (DLC). Readers gain insights into pursuing a career in game development and generating income through game sales.

38.9 Gaming Journalism and Content Creation: Gaming journalism and content creation provide avenues for individuals passionate about gaming to generate income through writing, podcasting, video production, and journalism. This section explores the world of gaming journalism, including writing reviews, news articles, and opinion pieces. It discusses the process of building a gaming-focused media platform, attracting readership, and monetizing content through advertising and partnerships. Readers gain insights into pursuing a career in gaming journalism.

38.10 Participating in Marketplaces and Trading: Online marketplaces and trading platforms provide opportunities for gamers to buy, sell, and trade in-game items, virtual currency, and collectibles. This section explores popular gaming marketplaces, such as Steam Community Market and PlayerAuctions, and the potential for income generation through item trading. It discusses strategies for identifying valuable in-game items, managing virtual inventories, and maximizing profits through trading. Readers gain insights into participating in gaming marketplaces as a source of income.

38.11 Hosting Gaming Events and Tournaments: Hosting gaming events and tournaments allows individuals to engage with the gaming community, build connections, and generate income through ticket sales, sponsorships, and advertising. This section explores the process of organizing gaming events, including planning, venue selection, logistics, and marketing. It discusses the potential for income generation through registration fees, partnerships with sponsors, and on-site sales. Readers gain insights into hosting successful gaming events.

38.12 Continuous Learning and Adaptation: Continuous learning and adaptation are essential in the ever-evolving world of online gaming and esports. This section emphasizes the importance of staying updated with gaming trends, new technologies, and emerging platforms. It discusses resources for ongoing education, such as game development courses, streaming tutorials, industry conferences, and online communities. Readers gain insights into cultivating a growth mindset, continuously improving their gaming skills, and adapting to changes in the gaming landscape.

By the end of Chapter 38, readers have gained a comprehensive understanding of generating income through online gaming and esports. They have explored various avenues, including esports competitions, game streaming, content creation, sponsorships, and merchandise sales. Armed with this knowledge, individuals passionate about gaming can confidently pursue income opportunities in the thriving world of online gaming and esports while building a fulfilling career in the industry.

CHAPTER 39: INNOVATING WITH ONLINE CROWDFUNDING AND FUNDRAISING

Chapter 39 explores the world of online crowdfunding and fundraising, providing readers with a comprehensive understanding of how individuals and organizations can leverage digital platforms to raise funds and bring innovative ideas to life. Online crowdfunding has revolutionized the way entrepreneurs, artists, non-profit organizations, and individuals can access capital and engage with a global community of supporters. This chapter serves as a guide, discussing different types of crowdfunding, strategies for successful campaigns, legal considerations, and innovative approaches to fundraising.

39.1 Introduction to Online Crowdfunding and Fundraising: This section introduces the concept of online crowdfunding and fundraising and highlights its transformative impact on the traditional fundraising landscape. It explores the democratization of funding, allowing individuals and organizations to raise capital directly from the public through online platforms. Readers gain insights into the advantages of online crowdfunding, such as expanded reach, increased transparency, and community engagement.

39.2 Understanding the Types of Crowdfunding: Crowdfunding encompasses various models, each with its unique characteristics and purposes. This section explores the different types of crowdfunding, including donation-based, reward-based, equity-based, and debt-based crowdfunding. It discusses how each model functions, the benefits it offers, and the legal considerations associated with each type. Readers gain insights into choosing the most suitable crowdfunding model for their specific goals and needs.

39.3 Setting Clear Fundraising Goals: Setting clear fundraising goals is crucial for a successful crowdfunding campaign. This section explores strategies for defining the purpose of the campaign, determining the funding target, and establishing realistic milestones. It discusses the importance of aligning goals with the project or cause and communicating them effectively to potential supporters. Readers gain insights into creating compelling narratives around their fundraising goals to inspire and engage backers.

39.4 Choosing the Right Crowdfunding Platform: Choosing the right crowdfunding platform is a critical decision that can impact the success of a fundraising campaign. This section explores popular crowdfunding platforms, such as Kickstarter, Indiegogo, GoFundMe, and Patreon. It discusses the features, fees, reach, and audience of each platform. Readers gain insights into selecting a platform that aligns with their fundraising goals, target audience, and project requirements.

39.5 Crafting a Compelling Crowdfunding Campaign: Crafting a compelling crowdfunding campaign is essential for capturing the attention and support of potential backers. This section explores strategies for creating a captivating campaign story, setting attractive rewards or perks for backers, and utilizing high-quality visuals and videos to convey the project's value. It discusses the importance of transparency, authenticity, and regular updates throughout the campaign. Readers gain insights into crafting a persuasive campaign that resonates with the target audience.

39.6 Engaging and Expanding the Supporter Base: Engaging and expanding the supporter base is key to the success of a crowdfunding campaign. This section explores strategies for reaching out to friends, family, and personal networks to secure initial support. It discusses techniques for utilizing social media, email marketing, and influencer collaborations to expand the campaign's reach. It also explores the importance of community engagement, fostering relationships with backers, and leveraging their networks for further support. Readers gain insights into building a strong support network for their crowdfunding campaign.

39.7 Leveraging Social Media and Online Marketing: Social media and online marketing play a significant role in the success of a crowdfunding campaign. This section explores strategies for creating a strong online presence, utilizing platforms like Facebook, Instagram, Twitter, and LinkedIn to promote the campaign, and engaging with potential backers. It discusses techniques for running targeted ads, partnering with influencers, and leveraging content marketing to generate interest and drive traffic to the campaign page. Readers gain insights into effective social media and online marketing strategies.

39.8 Building Trust and Credibility: Building trust and credibility are vital for encouraging individuals to contribute to a crowdfunding campaign. This section explores strategies for establishing credibility through transparent communication, providing regular updates on the project's progress, and showcasing the team's expertise and qualifications. It discusses the importance of testimonials, endorsements, and social proof in building trust. Readers gain insights into instilling confidence in potential backers and cultivating long-term relationships.

39.9 Legal Considerations and Compliance: Navigating the legal landscape is essential when conducting a crowdfunding campaign. This section explores legal considerations, including intellectual property rights, tax obligations, and compliance with crowdfunding regulations. It discusses the importance of clearly communicating the terms and conditions of the campaign and managing potential legal risks. Readers gain insights into seeking legal advice and ensuring compliance with relevant laws and regulations.

39.10 Innovative Approaches to Fundraising: Innovation is key to standing out in a competitive crowdfunding landscape. This section explores innovative approaches to fundraising, such as blockchain-based crowdfunding, equity crowdfunding for startups, and crowdfunding for social impact projects. It discusses the potential of emerging technologies, like decentralized finance (DeFi) and non-fungible tokens (NFTs), to revolutionize fundraising models. Readers gain insights into leveraging innovative strategies to differentiate their campaigns and attract backers.

39.11 Post-Campaign Fulfillment and Relationship Building: Post-campaign fulfillment and relationship building are critical for maintaining trust and credibility with backers. This section explores strategies for delivering rewards or perks to backers in a timely manner, providing regular updates on project milestones, and fostering ongoing communication with the supporter community. It discusses the importance of maintaining transparency, resolving any issues promptly, and expressing gratitude to backers. Readers gain insights into building long-lasting relationships with supporters beyond the campaign.

39.12 Continuous Learning and Adaptation: Continuous learning and adaptation are essential in the ever-evolving world of online crowdfunding and fundraising. This section emphasizes the importance of analyzing campaign data, evaluating outcomes, and learning from successes and failures. It discusses resources for ongoing education, such as crowdfunding courses, industry events, and networking opportunities. Readers gain insights into cultivating a growth mindset and continuously improving their crowdfunding and fundraising strategies.

By the end of Chapter 39, readers have gained a comprehensive understanding of innovating with online crowdfunding and fundraising. They have explored the different types of crowdfunding, learned strategies for successful campaigns, understood legal considerations, and discovered innovative approaches to fundraising. Armed with this knowledge, individuals and organizations can confidently leverage online platforms to raise funds, bring their ideas to life, and engage with a global community of supporters.

CHAPTER 40: BUILDING A SUSTAINABLE ONLINE BUSINESS FOR LONG-TERM SUCCESS

Chapter 40 explores the crucial aspect of building a sustainable online business for long-term success. While starting an online business can be exciting, it requires careful planning, strategic decision-making, and a focus on creating a solid foundation that can withstand the challenges and changes in the digital landscape. This chapter serves as a comprehensive guide, discussing key elements of building a sustainable online business, including business planning, customer-centric approach, effective operations, scalability, innovation, and long-term growth strategies.

40.1 Introduction to Building a Sustainable Online Business: This section introduces the concept of building a sustainable online business and highlights its significance in today's competitive digital landscape. It emphasizes the need for long-term thinking, resilience, and adaptability to create a business that can thrive over time. Readers gain insights into the benefits of building a sustainable online business, such as stability, profitability, and the ability to withstand market fluctuations.

40.2 Business Planning and Strategy: Effective business planning and strategy are fundamental to building a sustainable online business. This section explores the importance of defining a clear vision, mission, and goals for the business. It discusses the process of conducting market research, identifying target audiences, and understanding customer needs and preferences. Readers gain insights into developing a comprehensive business plan and defining strategies to achieve sustainable growth.

40.3 Customer-Centric Approach: A customer-centric approach is essential for building a sustainable online business. This section explores strategies for understanding customer behavior, gathering feedback, and delivering exceptional customer experiences. It discusses techniques for building relationships, implementing personalized marketing strategies, and creating a culture of customer-centricity within the organization. Readers gain insights into the importance of customer satisfaction, loyalty, and advocacy in long-term business success.

40.4 Effective Operations and Systems: Efficient operations and systems are crucial for the smooth functioning of an online business. This section explores strategies for streamlining processes, optimizing workflows, and utilizing technology to enhance productivity. It discusses the importance of implementing effective project management, inventory management, and customer relationship management systems. Readers gain insights into automating repetitive tasks, improving efficiency, and creating a scalable infrastructure for long-term growth.

40.5 Scalability and Flexibility: Scalability and flexibility are key considerations for building a sustainable online business. This section explores strategies for designing a business model that can adapt to changing market conditions and accommodate growth. It discusses the importance of scalability in product development, infrastructure, and customer acquisition strategies. Readers gain insights into leveraging technology, outsourcing non-core functions, and building partnerships to facilitate scalability and flexibility.

40.6 Innovation and Adaptation: Innovation and adaptation are vital for long-term success in the digital era. This section explores strategies for fostering a culture of innovation within the organization, encouraging creative thinking, and embracing emerging technologies and trends. It discusses the importance of staying updated with market dynamics, customer preferences, and industry advancements. Readers gain insights into implementing continuous improvement initiatives, experimenting with new ideas, and adapting to evolving customer needs.

40.7 Marketing and Branding for Long-Term Growth: Marketing and branding play a critical role in building a sustainable online business. This section explores strategies for developing a strong brand identity, positioning the business in the market, and creating effective marketing campaigns. It discusses techniques for utilizing digital marketing channels, content marketing, social media, and search engine optimization (SEO) to reach and engage target audiences. Readers gain insights into building brand equity, fostering customer loyalty, and driving long-term growth through effective marketing strategies.

40.8 Financial Management and Profitability: Effective financial management is essential for ensuring the long-term profitability and sustainability of an online business. This section explores strategies for budgeting, tracking expenses, managing cash flow, and optimizing revenue streams. It discusses the importance of monitoring key financial metrics, such as profit margins, return on investment (ROI), and customer lifetime value (CLV). Readers gain insights into financial planning, forecasting, and making informed financial decisions to support long-term business growth.

40.9 Building a Strong Team and Culture: Building a strong team and a positive organizational culture are integral to the sustainability of an online business. This section explores strategies for recruiting and retaining talented individuals who align with the company's values and vision. It discusses techniques for fostering collaboration, providing professional development opportunities, and promoting a supportive and inclusive work environment. Readers gain insights into building a high-performing team and nurturing a culture that drives long-term success.

40.10 Long-Term Growth Strategies: Long-term growth strategies are essential for sustained success in the online business landscape. This section explores strategies for expanding market reach, diversifying revenue streams, and entering new markets or niches. It discusses techniques for strategic partnerships, mergers and acquisitions, and product or service innovation. Readers gain insights into setting ambitious yet achievable growth targets and developing a roadmap to realize long-term business growth.

40.11 Continuous Learning and Adaptation: Continuous learning and adaptation are crucial for building a sustainable online business. This section emphasizes the importance of staying updated with industry trends, technological advancements, and customer preferences. It discusses resources for ongoing education, such as industry conferences, webinars, online courses, and networking opportunities. Readers gain insights into cultivating a growth mindset and continuously improving their business strategies to stay competitive in the digital landscape.

40.12 Embracing Social and Environmental Responsibility: Embracing social and environmental responsibility is a key aspect of building a sustainable online business. This section explores strategies for incorporating ethical practices, promoting sustainability, and contributing to social causes. It discusses techniques for reducing carbon footprint, supporting local communities, and engaging in corporate social responsibility (CSR) initiatives. Readers gain insights into building a business that not only focuses on profitability but also positively impacts society and the environment.

By the end of Chapter 40, readers have gained a comprehensive understanding of building a sustainable online business for long-term success. They have explored key elements such as business planning, customer-centricity, effective operations, scalability, innovation, long-term growth strategies, and social responsibility. Armed with this knowledge, entrepreneurs can confidently navigate the digital landscape, create a sustainable online business, and achieve long-term success in a rapidly evolving business environment.

EPILOGUE

Congratulations on reaching the end of "The Online Money Playbook: Mastering Advanced Online Money-Making Techniques." You've embarked on a journey to explore the vast opportunities presented by the digital landscape and have acquired the knowledge and strategies to harness the power of the internet for financial success. As you close this book, we encourage you to reflect on your accomplishments and embrace the possibilities that lie ahead.

The digital world is constantly evolving, and the techniques and platforms discussed in this book will continue to evolve as well. It is crucial to remain adaptable, open to learning, and willing to embrace new technologies and trends. The online money-making landscape is a dynamic one, presenting both opportunities and challenges. By staying informed and continuously expanding your skill set, you will position yourself for long-term success.

Remember that building a sustainable online business requires dedication, perseverance, and a customer-centric approach. As you venture into the online realm, focus on creating value, solving problems, and delivering exceptional experiences to your audience. Embrace innovation, experiment with new strategies, and constantly seek ways to improve and differentiate your offerings.

Throughout your online money-making journey, don't forget the importance of building meaningful connections and nurturing relationships. The power of collaboration, networking, and supporting others cannot be overstated. Engage with communities, join forums, attend industry events, and learn from others who share your passion. Together, we can create a supportive ecosystem where everyone can thrive.

As you move forward, be mindful of your goals and aspirations. Regularly reassess your progress, set new targets, and adjust your strategies accordingly. Remember that success is not solely measured by financial gains but also by the fulfillment and happiness derived from doing what you love and making a positive impact on others.

Lastly, as you build your online empire, remember to give back to the world that has provided you with abundant opportunities. Embrace social and environmental responsibility, contribute to causes that resonate with you, and use your platform to create positive change. By aligning your business endeavors with your values, you can make a meaningful difference while achieving personal and financial success.

"The Online Money Playbook: Mastering Advanced Online Money-Making Techniques" is not just a book; it is a roadmap to unlock your potential and realize your dreams. Remember that the knowledge and strategies shared within these pages are tools for empowerment, but it is your dedication, creativity, and perseverance that will shape your destiny.

We sincerely hope that this book has inspired you, provided you with valuable insights, and equipped you with the necessary tools to embark on a fulfilling and prosperous online money-making journey. Remember, the power to create your desired future lies within you.

Now, go forth and embrace the new era of online money-making. The digital world is waiting for your unique contributions, and the opportunities are boundless. Believe in yourself, stay committed to your vision, and keep pushing the boundaries of what is possible.

Thank you for joining us on this transformative journey. We wish you nothing but success, happiness, and abundance in all your online money-making endeavors.

Go make your mark on the digital world!